WALKING WITH PLATO

WALKING
WITH PLATO

A Philosophical Hike through the British Isles

Gary Hayden

WALKING WITH PLATO

A Philosophical Hike Through the British Isles

Gary Hayden

ONEWORLD

A Oneworld Book

First published in Great Britain, North America and
Australia by Oneworld Publications, 2016

ISBN 978-1-78074-656-2
eISBN 978-1-78074-657-9

Typeset by Hewer Text UK Ltd, Edinburgh

Printed and bound in Great Britain by Clays Ltd, St Ives plc

Oneworld Publications
10 Bloomsbury Street
London WC1B 3SR
England

For
everyone who helped us on our way.

Contents

Prologue

IT'S A BEAUTIFUL MID-JULY AFTERNOON. DOWN BELOW – and getting closer all the time – are the blue waters of the North Sea and the green moorland pastures of the northeast Highlands.

The tiny propeller-plane is bouncing around and making whining noises. So, to take my mind off the bouncing and the whining, I do some mental arithmetic: *There are two thousand steps in a mile. So that's two million steps in a thousand miles. But we'll probably do nearer to twelve hundred miles. So that's two-and-a-half million steps, as near as dammit.*

Soon, we'll land in Wick. From there, we'll take a bus to John o'Groats. And tomorrow, we'll start walking to Land's End.

Wendy, sitting beside me, is looking happy and serene.

'Do you realize, we're going to be walking two-and-a-half *million* steps?' I say.

She ponders the information for a moment, then grins and says, 'Brilliant!'

I lean back in my seat and wonder what the hell I've let myself in for.

The fact is, I've always been a reluctant walker. In the early days of our marriage, I would sometimes accompany Wendy on mountain-walks in Snowdonia or the Lake District. But I'd usually get bored and grumpy within a few hours. So eventually she gave up on me and joined a walking group.

Since hitting middle age, I've become more tolerant of perambulatory excursions. They're good exercise, if nothing else. But, on the whole, I've still tended to view walking as a rather dull affair.

On the face of it, then, I'm an unlikely candidate for the 'End to End': Britain's longest long-distance walking challenge, extending from the northeastern tip of Scotland to the southwestern tip of England. But I was prompted to it by two considerations.

First and foremost, Wendy wanted to do it. In fact, she'd wanted to do it for years. And now, at the end of a five-year stint teaching in an international school in Ho Chi Minh City, Vietnam, she'd finally found the time.

Second, I'm a sucker for a physical challenge. Like many middle-aged men, I'm engaged in a constant, bitter, and losing battle against physical decline. This means that, when I'm not devouring pasties and guzzling beer, I take grim pleasure in making my paunchy body run around, do press-ups, and perform tricks with a skipping-rope. So, in that sense, a three-month hike up and down hills carrying a heavy rucksack is right up my street.

For those reasons, when Wendy suggested End to Ending, I surprised her by saying yes.

Even so, I still had my doubts about the whole thing. After all, three months is a long time; and twelve hundred miles is a long way; and two-and-a-half million steps – that's an *awful* lot of steps.

The plane continues its bumpy descent. I look out of the window, and I have to admit that those blue waters and green pastures *do* look inviting.

So who knows? Wendy might be right. It could just turn out to be brilliant . . .

The beginning is the most
important part of any work.

———

—PLATO, *REPUBLIC*

CHAPTER ONE

First Steps

*John o'Groats – Duncansby Head – Wick –
Dunbeath – Berriedale – Helmsdale – Brora –
Golspie – Dornoch Firth – Evanton – Inverness*

THERE'S NO SET ROUTE FOR THE END TO END. YOU CAN DO it entirely along roads or you can navigate your way through forest, field, and mountain. You can take a more or less straight line or you can zigzag around, stopping off anywhere that takes your fancy. You can do it from Land's End to John o'Groats (LEJoG) or you can do it – as Wendy and I did – from John o'Groats to Land's End (JoGLE). You can take as much or as little time over it as you like.

All that matters is that you walk every step of the way.

If you take the direct(ish) route, along roads, the journey is about 850 miles, which means that you can do it in six weeks or less if you hoof it.

Most End to Enders, however, opt for a more scenic route, taking long-distance paths whenever possible and using roads only when necessary. These journeys are typically between eleven hundred and twelve hundred miles long, and take two to three months to complete.

Wendy and I planned to take a scenic route along some of Britain's best-loved National Trails, including the Great Glen

Way, the West Highland Way, the Pennine Way, the Heart of England Way, the Cotswold Way, and the South West Coast Path.

The first of these, the Great Glen Way, begins at Inverness, Scotland's most northerly city, which is situated 120 miles south of John o'Groats.

For the End to Ender, there are two ways of getting from John o'Groats to Inverness. You can loop west through some of the most remote parts of the Scottish Highlands, wild-camp beneath the stars, and experience Nature at her most wild and free. Or you can trudge 120 miles along the A99 and the A9, dodge traffic, trash the soles of your feet, and endure hour upon hour of mind-numbing tedium.

Wendy and I chose the latter option.

Here's the journey in a nutshell.

You walk 118 miles by road: first from John o'Groats to Dunbeath along the A99, and then from Dunbeath to Inverness along the A9. Sometimes you have the sea on your left and rough pasture on your right. Sometimes, when the road takes you further inland, you have rough pasture on both your left *and* your right.

Sometimes, you pass through a small town or a tiny village. Occasionally, you come across a museum or a quaint harbour or a nice little beach. Every so often, you get to take a brief but delicious detour along a minor road or down a forest track. But for the most part you just plod along the A-road.

Sometimes the road is busy and wide and dangerous. At other times it is quiet and narrow and dangerous. There's rarely a footpath.

If, like Wendy and me, your budget doesn't stretch to B&Bs, then you sometimes have to walk long distances to get from one campsite to the next, unless you are the adventurous type and don't mind wild-camping in a farmer's field at the side of the road.

This means that unless you are wealthy or intrepid you never get time to explore the towns and villages, or to visit the museums and harbours and beaches. You're too busy hurrying on.

You wake up. You take down your tent. You walk. You set up your tent. You sleep. Apart from eating, that's pretty much it.

For the first day or two, you make an effort to look around as you walk: at the sea to your left and the rough pasture to your right. But you soon give up the effort. Your eyes are irresistibly drawn to the road.

Our first day's walk took us from our guesthouse in **John o'Groats** to nearby **Duncansby Head** and back again: a round-trip of about six miles.

In 2010, John o'Groats won (but refused to accept) a Carbuncle Award from *Urban Realm* magazine for being 'Scotland's most dismal town'. I have nothing to add except that it serves what is quite possibly Scotland's most dismal fish and chips from a portakabin overlooking the harbour.

Uninhabited Duncansby Head, the most northeasterly point on the Scottish mainland, and the true start/finish of the End to End challenge, is a whole other kettle of fish. With its tiny lighthouse, sea cliffs, comical puffins, sea-breezes, and stacks (large pinnacles of rock jutting out from the sea), it puts its better-known near-neighbour to shame.

On our second day, Wendy and I shouldered our backpacks (complete with tent, sleeping-mats, sleeping-bags, pillows, clothing, waterproofs, cooking equipment, toiletries, torches, first-aid kit, electronic items, and food and water) and hit the road with a vengeance.

Eight hours and sixteen miles later, we reached **Wick**, a fair-sized estuary town, which was once a major player in the herring industry.

Wick, for all I know, may have its attractions. But for me, that day, aching and weary as I was, it was nothing more than a final obstacle en route to our campsite on the outskirts of the farther side of town.

By the end of the third day – twenty hot and dusty miles from Wick to the coastal village of **Dunbeath** – I was literally groaning with pain.

Two days of carrying a thirty-five-pound rucksack had taken such a toll on my shoulders and back that I grunted and squirmed and cursed my way along the last few miles to our campsite.

Wendy, by this time limping ten or fifteen yards behind me, was in an even worse condition. Constant pounding of the tarmac road had blistered her toes so badly that they barely looked like toes any more. Every step was a triumph of will – and stupidity – over pain.

I had known beforehand that the End to End would be no picnic, that there would be times when weary muscles, sore feet, and sheer bloody tedium would test our mettle and resolve. But I had anticipated neither how quickly nor how severely we would be tested.

When I had looked ahead, in my mind's eye, at the trials and tribulations we would face, they had all seemed rather romantic. I had pictured myself battling through them with a stern and manly look on my face. But I learned very quickly that there is nothing romantic about an aching back and sore feet.

During the afternoon of that third gruelling day, as I dragged myself along the dreary ribbon of tarmac that is the A9, I kept up my flagging spirits by ruminating on some wise words from the pen of the English philosopher Bertrand Russell: 'The secret of happiness is to understand that the world is horrible, horrible, horrible.'

At first glance, those words appear facetious: a paradoxical *bon mot* intended for amusement rather than edification. But the more you think about them, the more you realize that they are as true as they are witty, and as wise as they are true.

Take JoGLE, for example. If you set off expecting three months of jolly jaunts through the British countryside, then you're going to be sorely disappointed. You'll quickly discover that it's not all lighthouses and puffins and sea-breezes.

On the contrary, if you're going to walk all the way from John o'Groats to Land's End, then, as sure as eggs is eggs, you'll have to endure sore feet, aching limbs, inclement weather, fatigue, accidents, disappointments, and boredom. Sometimes you'll feel like jacking the whole thing in.

But, if you know all of this beforehand, if you understand that it comes with the territory, then you can keep going. You can say to yourself, 'This was only to be expected.'

This is especially true of the A99/A9 section between John o'Groats and Inverness. Every End to Ender who's done even a modicum of research knows that it's long, it's tedious, and it's tough on your feet. So the best thing to do is to accept it; roll with it; suck it up. Because if you hang in long enough you'll eventually get back to the good stuff: to the lighthouses, the puffins, and the sea-breezes.

And it's the same with life, in general. If you blunder your way through it thinking that the world owes you or anyone else a good time, you'll be sorely disappointed. Every time you're rejected, betrayed, or frustrated, every time you encounter pain or sickness, every time you're cheated, mistreated, or defeated, you'll feel angry and aggrieved.

But if you accept that the world cares nothing for you and your plans, that it's a pitiless place where bad things happen even to good people, never mind the likes of you and me, then when bad things *do* happen you can accept them stoically and wait – or, at any rate, *hope* – for better times.

And the good news is that for most of us, most of the time, better times do come around eventually.

I was painfully conscious, as we squirmed and grunted and limped our way to Reception at the Inver Caravan Park in Dunbeath, of what a pathetic spectacle we made. But I could sum up neither the will nor the energy to try to appear anything other than I truly was: knackered.

The owner greeted us with a look of pity. She asked if we were by any chance heading for Land's End, and then comforted us by observing that she had known people arrive 'in an even worse condition'.

An hour later, having erected our backpacker tent and abandoned plans to cook dinner on our camping stove, we hobbled our way to the nearby Bay Owl pub: an ugly flat-roofed concrete building with a surprisingly good restaurant and a fine view of Dunbeath Harbour and Castle.

I knew that bad times had temporarily given way to good the moment I looked towards the bar and saw a shiny brass hand-pump, all primed and ready to deliver Trade Winds real ale.

If you have never drunk a pint of beer after toiling footsore and weary along thirty-six miles of hot and dusty road, then you can have no inkling of how good that beer tasted. It quenched my thirst; it nourished my body; it restored my spirits; it uplifted my soul.

It was more than a drink. It was consolation. It was courage. It was hope.

Consolation, courage, and hope were further restored by chips, steak-and-ale pie, and an additional half-pint of Trade Winds. Within the hour, I was able to look back with amused complacency upon the trials and tribulations of the previous two days. I began to feel that every single body-bruising mile had been worthwhile, that, without the toil, the sweat, and the pain, I might never have appreciated the true worth of a good pint of ale.

Like many people who live in the developed world, I rarely get to appreciate food and drink properly, because I rarely sit down to a meal feeling weary and hungry, and having worked physically hard for it.

But that day, having pushed myself harder and for longer than ever before, I was primed for enjoyment. In addition to the usual pleasures of the table – the taste, texture, and aroma of the food and the gentle satisfaction of a full stomach – there was the added thrill of refuelling the muscles and the mind.

The feeling is hard to explain, but it's as though every tired and depleted cell in your body is sucking up energy and sustenance as you eat and drink. And it's sublime.

In the absence of this pleasure, we in the developed world tend to seek our culinary kicks in mere excess. Step into any Starbucks or Costa Coffee and you'll see what I mean: overweight, under-exercised punters ramming down 'coffees' laced with flavoured syrups and whipped cream, accompanied by a side-helping of cheesecake and a dollop of self-loathing.

As I sat there musing upon all of this, I began to appreciate what the Ancient Greek philosopher Epicurus meant when he wrote to a friend: 'Living on bread and water, I rejoice in the pleasure of my body and spit upon the pleasures of extravagance.'

I had thought about those words often before, and had even written about them, but only at that moment did I feel that I truly understood them.

Epicurus had shunned urban life and had set up a self-sufficient community outside the walls of Athens. This meant that when he sat down to his bread and water at the end of each working day he was primed for enjoyment. He was weary and hungry, and had worked physically hard for them.

This is why his simple fare 'thrilled him with pleasure in the body', and why he was able to write to the same friend: 'Send me a little vessel of cheese, so that I can feast whenever I please.'

I had always assumed that Epicurus's ability to enjoy a modest diet came about as a result of mental discipline, that he had somehow *willed* himself to appreciate it. But, no. It was a natural consequence of his back-to-the-land, hard-working way of life.

That night, cramped up in our tiny backpacker tent, we examined Wendy's feet by torchlight.

Her blisters had ballooned so much that the two smallest toes on each foot looked like fluid-filled sausage-skins with toenails glued none-too-securely onto the ends. It was clear that it would be an act of folly to squeeze them into hiking boots and beat them against an unforgiving road any time soon. There was nothing for it but to hole up in Dunbeath and let Nature practise her healing arts.

The next morning, as I sat in Dunbeath's cosy little tea-room, eating jam-and-cream scones, I couldn't help but notice a certain restiveness about Wendy.

My first thought was that this was because our unscheduled stop was taking us off timetable and over budget. So I felt a twinge of irritation. Why couldn't she just relax and enjoy the moment?

But then I fancied I caught a look in her eye, which aroused my sympathy.

I have a distinct memory, from when I was about eight or nine years old, of standing at the window, at home, looking out into the street, and longing – literally *longing* – for someone to play chess with.

I had recently learned how to play, and had borrowed a bunch of chess books from the library, but I had no one to play *with*. And it was torment.

Perhaps it was my imagination, but it seemed to me that Wendy, as she gazed out of the tea-room window, was feeling the same way. Not that she wanted to play chess, of course. But she was longing to be *out there*.

The nineteenth-century American psychologist and philosopher William James wrote:

I have often thought that the best way to define a man's character would be to seek out the particular mental or moral attitude in which, when it came upon him, he felt himself most deeply and intensely active and alive. At such moments there is a voice inside which speaks and says: 'This is the real me!'

If that's true – and I believe it is – then it's the easiest thing in the world to define Wendy's character.

Wendy is, at heart, a wild woman.

She is never more active and never more alive than when she is striding along a mountain track with the wind in her hair.

I often think that what she really ought to be doing with her life is digging wells in Africa, or rehabilitating gibbons in Thailand, or fighting bush fires in Australia. But instead, she's a teacher. She's a committed one, and a caring one, and a good one. But, in my opinion, it's not really her.

And there she was, after five years cooped up in a classroom, longing to roam, and having to sit cooped up in a café, gazing out upon it all.

It was four whole days before she was ready to walk again.

That was fine by me. We had arrived in the far north of Scotland in the middle of a heatwave, which was as conducive to lounging around on a campsite as it was non-conducive to lumbering along an A-road.

I remarked earlier that the End to Ender gets little time to explore the museums and harbours and beaches along the road from John o'Groats to Inverness. But we had oodles of time to do those things at Dunbeath.

We picnicked at its sleepy little harbour, mooched around its sleepy little museum, visited its sleepy little heritage centre, and drank real ale, each evening, in the Bay Owl's sleepy little bar-room.

I enjoyed it all immensely. But for Wendy's sake I wasn't sorry, on the fifth evening, when the Bay Owl's landlord asked, 'Have ye no' gone yet?' to be able to respond, 'No. But we'll be leaving in the morning.'

When we eventually hit the road again, we understood our limitations. We weren't yet strong enough, or tough enough or fit enough to string together twenty-mile walks. Not with backpacks, anyway.

So we scrapped the punishing schedule we had set ourselves, and opted instead for a few days of short sensible walks: eight miles to Berriedale, then eight miles to Helmsdale, and then nine miles to Brora.

We walked the first section, between Dunbeath and the tiny village of **Berriedale**, in reverse. Keith and Rona, the retirement-aged proprietors of the Inver Caravan Park, drove us to a layby on the A9, just past Berriedale, and from there we returned, on foot but without backpacks, to the campsite in Dunbeath.

Apart from an outrageously steep section of road just north of Berriedale (a 13% incline over 0.8 miles), and the fact that it poured down with rain whenever we *weren't* wearing our waterproofs and turned hot and sunny whenever we *were* wearing them, it was a nice easy reintroduction to the trail.

The following morning, Keith and Rona drove us back to the same layby, and waved us goodbye as we ventured onwards – this time, alas, *with* backpacks – to the fishing port of **Helmsdale**.

The A9 hugs the side of some coastal hills here, which makes for some pretty scenery. But it was wasted on us. We were too busy hopping on and off the narrow, litter-strewn verge, dodging traffic, to take much notice of it.

There's no campsite at Helmsdale. So we had to splash out on a B&B. This was a splendid treat even though we couldn't really afford it.

From Helmsdale we walked nine miles, with the sea to our left and moorland hills to our right, to a beachside campsite just outside the village of **Brora**.

It's impossible to walk along the A9 and remain interested in the world around you. Your eyes get drawn downward, to the road.

And when your eyes are drawn downward, your thoughts turn inward. This is all very well if you're the cheerful, happy-go-lucky type who thinks cheerful, happy-go-lucky thoughts. But if you're the brooding, introspective type, it can be a problem.

Personally, I'm the brooding, introspective type. So my natural tendency, when my eyes are glued to a tarmac road, is to depress the hell out of myself.

I'll look back at every dumb, misguided thing I've ever done, and I'll replay it and replay it. Then I'll replay it some more with variations – usually involving a wiser, better me who does everything so much better, second time around.

It's a bad habit. It's unhealthy. It's unhelpful. It's depressing. But it's strangely addictive.

Bertrand Russell discusses this kind of introspection and its pernicious consequences in the opening chapter of his 1930 book *The Conquest of Happiness*. He opens the discussion by describing how unhappy he was as a child:

> At the age of five, I reflected that, if I should live to be seventy, I had only endured, so far, a fourteenth part of my whole life, and I felt the long-spread-out boredom ahead of me to be almost unendurable.

By the time he reached adolescence, he hated life so much that he often contemplated suicide. But, despite this inauspicious beginning, he learned to enjoy life as he grew older, and attributed this largely to a diminishing preoccupation with himself. Whereas in his youth he would brood upon his faults and failings and make himself thoroughly miserable, as an adult he learned to fix his attention on external things such as world affairs, various branches of knowledge, and other people.

He writes:

> External interests, it is true, bring each its own possibility of pain: the world may be plunged in war, knowledge in some direction may be hard to achieve, friends may die. But pains of these kinds do not destroy the essential quality of life, as do those that spring from disgust with self.

I know from my own experience, and not merely upon Russell's authority, that external interests are key to happiness, and that the times when I have thrown myself wholeheartedly into computer programming, or teaching, or philosophy, or writing, or even chasing a rubber ball around a squash court have been the best times in my life.

But, unlike Russell, I never did kick the habit of brooding. In fact, as I have grown older, I have found myself, more and more, whenever I have leisure to think, ruminating upon my faults and failings, and falling prey to self-disgust.

So, for me, pounding along the A9, staring for hours at a ribbon of tarmac, wasn't an uplifting experience. Nor, I'm sure, did it make me the most pleasant and stimulating of companions.

From Brora, we walked six or seven miles to the coastal village of **Golspie**.

We'd intended to walk eighteen miles to Dornoch that day. But Wendy's blisters would have none of it. So at eleven o'clock we stopped at Golspie, rang around, and found a room at a B&B.

We were checked in by midday, and able to enjoy a picnic lunch and a long lazy afternoon at Golspie's attractive little harbour and beach.

The next day, we managed a seventeen-mile hike to a campsite on the southern shore of **Dornoch Firth**.

Happily, we were able to detour off the A9 and onto small

country roads for much of the day, including a delicious three-mile section along the shore of Loch Fleet. This beautiful sea loch with its mudflats, wading birds, wildfowl, and basking seals was a slice of heaven – and a harbinger of better things to come.

From Dornoch Firth, we hiked eighteen miles to the village of **Evanton**.

Once again, we were able to leave the A9 and walk along minor roads, through woodland and farmland, for much of the day. It would have been quite pleasant had the weather not been so energy-sappingly hot, and had my feet not, by then, become so tender.

By four o'clock, when we passed through the small town of Alness, our mental and physical reserves were sorely depleted. Yet we still had four miles to go.

We dragged our tired bodies into a café, flopped down at a table, and ordered coffee and shortbread. Thirty minutes later, we emerged – to my astonishment – with renewed vigour. I never dreamed that a brief sit down, a hot drink, and a couple of biscuits could work such magic.

Sadly, further trials awaited us.

Half a mile further on, the heavens opened. Within minutes, the dry and dusty road had turned into a shallow stream, and the gutters had become a torrent. Passing traffic sent waves five feet high crashing over us.

We battled through this deluge for a few hundred yards, and

then stopped to hold crisis talks in the scanty shelter of a bus-stop. Clearly, this wasn't camping weather. But what should we do? Should we stop and try to find a B&B? Or should we press on and hope there was room in the bunkhouse at the Evanton campsite?

We elected to press on.

We arrived to find a fully occupied bunkhouse and a sodden campsite. Everything – the grass, the trees, the caravans, the campervans, the bunkhouse, the laundry, and the children's playground – was wet through and dripping, in the dreariest manner imaginable, with water.

Wettest of all was the field set aside for tents, which, for reasons I can't fathom, was situated at the bottom of a small incline.

The tents already pitched there lay in puddles two inches deep. A group of children in waterproofs and wellies were using the field as a paddling pool. And all the while the rain continued to pour down.

The situation appeared hopeless. Luckily, however, the guy who ran the campsite came along and pointed to a small patch of ground at the top of the incline, upon which it might just be possible to squeeze our backpacker tent.

It was wet and muddy, and it was getting wetter and muddier by the minute, but it wasn't actually submerged.

Grasping at this straw, Wendy and I set up a base of operations in the camp's laundry room, and spent the next hour running to and fro with bits of tent and camping equipment. Eventually, we managed to set up a passably dry shelter, and, after strewing our wet clothes around the laundry room to dry, passed a not entirely uncomfortable night.

I recall listening to the *Philosophy Talk* radio show once, and one of the hosts, either John Perry or Ken Taylor, remarked that one of the most important things he had learned during the course of his life is that 'good times never last and neither do bad times'.

This phrase became something of a mantra to me as I walked, often wearily and sometimes painfully, along the road to Inverness.

Whenever the going got tough – whenever my muscles ached, or my feet hurt, or my energy levels dropped, or my spirits flagged – I reminded myself that bad times don't last.

I felt that this first, tough section of JoGLE – and, quite possibly, JoGLE as a whole – could be seen as a microcosm of human life in its constant switching back and forth between hardship and comfort, toil and repose, pain and pleasure.

The nineteenth-century German philosopher Arthur Schopenhauer, in his masterwork *The World as Will and Representation*, gave a striking illustration of the human condition. He said that we can think of our journey through life as being like 'a circle of hot coals having a few cool places, a path that we have to run over incessantly'.

His point, in keeping with his reputation as the most pessimistic of philosophers, was a negative one. Namely that lasting happiness is impossible, that the best that life has to offer is the occasional period of respite from the pain of unfulfilled desire.

But, as I limped along the final stages of our journey to Inverness, I thought of Schopenhauer's circle in a more positive way. Whenever I got tired, or sore, or fed up, I would picture myself passing over the hot coals, and think, *there's a cool patch just around the bend!*

And, surprisingly enough, that thought was sufficient to make the hard times feel not merely bearable, but also – in a weird kind of a way – worthwhile.

When walking from Evanton to **Inverness**, it's possible, with some straightforward rerouting, to avoid a big stretch of the A9 and take small roads and cycle routes instead. Wendy and I decided not to do that – though I can't remember why.

Perhaps it was because my feet had, by this time, become agonizingly tender, making me want to complete the journey using the most direct route possible. Whatever the reason, it was an excruciatingly dull seventeen-mile walk, enlivened only by the crossing, early in the day, of the mile-long Cromarty Bridge, which spans Cromarty Firth.

The last few miles, along the A9 into Inverness, and then through the city centre to our campsite on the farther side of town, were the most dispiriting and painful of JoGLE so far.

The final section of A-road is a drab, multi-lane affair. Bearable enough, I suppose, if you're hurtling along in an air-conditioned vehicle with your favourite tunes blasting out of the stereo. But depressing as hell if you're crazy enough to be walking the damn thing: grunting under the weight of a fully laden rucksack as you make your way along a grass verge littered with cigarette butts, fag packets, crisp bags, plastic bags, empty beer cans, spat-out chewing gum, McDonald's packaging, and soiled disposable nappies.

More depressing still when you realize that it's a full hour since you first caught sight of the city, and yet you seem to be no closer to it now than you were back then.

More depressing still when you realize that you still have three miles to go, and your feet are already so sore that you can hardly bring yourself to take another step.

More depressing still when you finally get to the campsite where you are to spend the night and realize that it's an ugly compound, surrounded by an enormous security fence, in a seedy part of town.

All of that aside, Inverness is a splendid city. A 2014 survey identified it as the happiest (and therefore, I suppose, in some sense, the nicest) place in Scotland.

It has a lot going for it. It's picturesquely sited at the mouth of the River Ness, and it has a magnificent crenelated castle, a historic Old Town, a Victorian market, and oodles of riverside restaurants and pavement cafés.

More importantly, for cash-strapped backpackers like Wendy and me, who need somewhere to sit, cheap food, free

Wi-Fi, and a socket to charge their electronic devices, it has a Wetherspoon's.

We spent a much-needed rest day in Inverness: eating and drinking, buying gel-insoles for our hiking boots, and preparing ourselves physically and mentally to go off-road, onto the trail, and into the wild heart of the Scottish Highlands.

How singular is the thing called pleasure, and how curiously related to pain, which might be thought to be the opposite of it; for they are never present to a man at the same instant, and yet he who pursues either is generally compelled to take the other; their bodies are two, but they are joined by a single head.

—PLATO, *PHAEDO*

CHAPTER TWO

Simple Pleasures

Inverness – Drumnadrochit – Fort Augustus –
South Laggan – Gairlochy – Fort William

THE GREAT THING ABOUT DOING JoGLE, AS OPPOSED TO
LEJoG, is that you get the nasty bit out of the way at the very
beginning.

As JoGLErs, Wendy and I left **Inverness** with the worst of
the tarmac and the traffic and the tedium behind us, and with
some of Britain's finest long-distance footpaths ahead of us.
LEJoGers, on the other hand, leave Inverness with all of the
good stuff behind them, and with nothing but tarmac and traffic and tedium between them and their journey's end.

It was with high hopes, then, that we set off along the Great
Glen Way on the second stage of our End to End adventure.

The Great Glen Way is a seventy-nine-mile walking trail that
runs along the Great Glen: a geological fault line extending
from Inverness on Scotland's northeast coast to Fort William on
the southwest.

Although the trail runs through the Highlands, it keeps
mainly to low ground, sticking pretty closely to the line of the

Caledonian Canal. Along the way, it traverses the lengths of Loch Ness, Loch Oich, and Loch Lochy, linking these with sections of woodland, moorland, and canal towpath.

Since opening in 2002, the Great Glen Way has garnered mixed reviews from walkers. Some rave about the views of Lochs Ness, Oich, and Lochy; others complain that too much time is spent on forest paths where there is nothing to see but trees. Some enjoy strolling, deep in reverie, along the peaceful canal paths; others find the long stretches of towpath monotonous. Some revel in the solitude and tranquillity of the trail; others bemoan the dearth of accommodation, pubs, and teashops.

But every seasoned walker will agree that the worst day on the Great Glen Way is incomparably better than the best day on the road between John o'Groats and Inverness.

Our destination, that first day on the Great Glen Way, was the Highland village of **Drumnadrochit**. Our eighteen-mile route lay mostly through moorland and forest, with a final stretch alongside the west shore of Loch Ness.

Partway through the morning, when we had left the last traces of urban life behind, I paused to take a photograph of Wendy.

I'm looking at that photograph as I write.

She is standing on a narrow path surrounded by rough grass and slender trees. The trees nearest to the path are bent over so that their leafy branches form a natural archway. A fine mist hangs in the air.

She is dressed in walking trousers, technical T-shirt, and hiking boots. She has a rucksack on her back and walking poles dangling from her wrists. She is eating nuts.

It struck me then – and it strikes me now – that this was, and is, the real Wendy, that the workaday, lesson-planning, form-filling, report-writing, nine-to-five Wendy is a mere shadow of the woodland Wendy.

In *The Conquest of Happiness*, Bertrand Russell describes seeing a London child taken out for the first time into the countryside: 'In the boy there sprang up a strange ecstasy; he kneeled in the wet ground and put his face in the wet grass, and gave utterance to half-articulate cries of delight.'

The child's joy, which Russell describes as 'primitive, simple and massive', seemed to be at work in Wendy: softening her features, brightening her eyes, and placing the hint of a smile permanently upon her lips. Suddenly, I felt glad – heartily, almost tearfully, glad – to be there.

Later, on a secluded section of the Abriachan Forest, two-thirds of the way to Drumnadrochit, we came across a wooden post with the words 'CAFE & CAMPSITE' painted on it.

As we walked on, we came across more signs, all hand-painted, dotted at intervals along the path. Some of them promised 'REFRESHMENTS', 'HOT CHOCOLATE', 'COFFEE', 'TOASTIES', and suchlike; others offered words of encouragement such as 'OPEN', '365 DAYS', and 'ALMOST THERE . . .'

They were a welcome sight, especially since we now had persistent rain as well as sore feet to contend with. But they also had a somewhat sinister air. The forest seemed such a remote and unlikely place to house a café that I couldn't quite shake off the feeling that we were being lured into a trap.

I told Wendy that, if the café turned out to be made of gingerbread, or if there were any chainsaws thereabouts, we ought to keep right on walking.

As it turned out, the café did exist, and it wasn't made of gingerbread. But it did have a clonking great buzz-saw lying around.

The word 'café' is actually rather misleading. It suggests a building of some kind, with tables and chairs, and a kitchen and a counter-top. Whereas, in fact, it was just a ramshackle collection of sheds and outhouses in the grounds of someone's partially built eco-friendly home.

The coffee, which came with complimentary shortbread biscuits, was good though – and all the better for being served in non-matching crockery by the good-natured eco-homesteaders, Howie and Sandra.

As I sat slurping coffee, munching shortbread, and ignoring the hungry looks of the farm dogs, I thought again about Epicurus, and about the intense delight that simple pleasures can bring.

In his *Letter to Menoeceus*, Epicurus wrote: 'Bread and water confer the highest possible pleasure when they are brought to hungry lips.'

Of course, you don't need to be a philosopher to understand that bread tastes great when you're hungry and that water tastes great when you're thirsty. But Epicurus understood something more than that. He also understood that the converse is true, that the most sumptuous fare ceases to give pleasure when it's too abundantly available.

I can vouch for that.

Before setting off on JoGLE, Wendy and I lived for five years in Ho Chi Minh City, Vietnam, a city where it's possible to live very well on an ordinary ex-pat salary.

In the UK, an international buffet with free-flowing champagne at a posh hotel would be out of the reach of people like us. But in Ho Chi Minh City it's really quite affordable. Consequently, we ended up doing 'free-flow brunch' quite often, whenever we had visitors, or whenever a friend had something to celebrate.

The first time I sat down to champagne, lobster, and whatnot in a plush hotel, I felt as though I'd died and gone to heaven. But, after I'd done it every couple of months for five years, it ceased to be very exciting. Certainly less exciting than coffee and shortbread at the Abriachan Café. And I have no doubt that, if you did free-flow brunch every day, it would cease to be exciting at all.

This is a specific instance of the general truth that the more you have, the less you appreciate it. A truth that prompted Epicurus to write, in a letter to his disciple Idomeneus: 'If you wish to make Pythocles rich, do not add to his store of money, but subtract from his desires.'

So, when Epicurus and his disciples devoted themselves to a back-to-nature lifestyle, and to a simple, wholesome diet, it wasn't because they thought there was any virtue in denying themselves pleasure. Quite the contrary. It was because they wanted to *maximize* the amount of pleasure in their lives.

They wanted to sit down each evening to enjoy the intense pleasure that wholesome food brings to a tired and hungry body. And when the occasional treat came their way ('Send me a little vessel of cheese, so that I can feast whenever I please'), they wanted to relish it to the full, with unjaded appetites.

So, as Wendy and I left the Abriachan Café behind, and walked once more past its curious assortment of half-welcoming, half-scary signs, I thought that perhaps Howie and Sandra ought to add one more sign to their collection: one with the same message that Epicurus's disciples placed at the entrance to their garden.

This garden will not tease your appetite with the dainties of art but satisfy it with the bounties of nature.

The vision of Wendy at her wild and wonderful best, and the Epicurean delights of the Abriachan Café, had got my first morning in the Highlands off to a cheerful start. But as the afternoon wore on, and as the minutes passed more and more slowly, I began to feel a familiar sense of ennui.

I found the walking pleasant. But I didn't find it nearly stim-ulating enough. I found myself wishing the day away: counting the hours until we reached Drumnadrochit. Even worse, I found myself wishing JoGLE away: counting the days and weeks until we reached Land's End.

A few miles from Drumnadrochit, the trail dropped down out of the trees and gave us our first unobstructed view of Loch Ness: a long expanse of water, lying serenely between the hills, forests, and fields of the glen.

But footsoreness, weariness, and boredom had blunted my appetite for nature. Not even Loch Ness, the most famous of all lochs, the second-largest lake in Britain, and the stomping ground of Nessie, the Loch Ness Monster, could hold my attention.

We plodded on for a mile or two along the banks of the loch, and then turned inland along the final stretch into Drumnadrochit.

Drumnadrochit is a pleasant, touristy village. Its attractions include a Loch Ness museum, something called Nessieland ('an exciting new interesting, systematic, formulated and factual exhibition on Loch Ness', apparently), and the magnificent ruins of nearby Urquhart Castle.

But for Wendy and me, with our tight schedule and our even tighter budget, its one unmissable attraction was the Drum Takeaway: a great-value fish-and-chip shop, which we stopped at en route to our campsite, just outside town.

The following morning, we could have opted, as many walkers do, for a modest fourteen-mile loch-side walk from Drumnadrochit to the village of Invermoriston. But instead, mindful of the five days we'd lost at Dunbeath, and strangely unmindful of our battered feet and heavy rucksacks, we plumped for a twenty-two-mile forced march to **Fort Augustus**.

It was a splendid day, full of sunshine and birdsong. The trail, which lay close to the west shore of Loch Ness, offered some glorious sights: wild expanses of moorland strewn with yellow-flowering broom, shady forest paths dappled with sunlight, rugged hills clothed in a patchwork of light-green meadow and dark-green forest, and the grey-blue ribbon of the loch itself, stretching out along the contour of the glen.

It was a day – if ever there was one – for experiencing the 'primitive, simple and massive' joy that contact with nature can bring. In fact, looking back now, in my mind's eye, at the yellow-flowering broom and the dappled forest paths and the grey-blue ribbon of the loch, I feel a kind of joy.

But at the time it was largely lost on me because of my feet.

In John Bunyan's seventeenth-century religious and literary masterpiece *The Pilgrim's Progress*, there's a passage in which the hero, Christian, and his companion, Hopeful, stray from the straight and narrow way that leads to the Celestial City.

Footsore and weary, they turn aside from their rough and stony path to tread for a while upon soft green meadows.

But, in departing from the Way, they unwittingly trespass upon the lands of Giant Despair, a pitiless monster who imprisons them in his dungeon in Doubting Castle and starves and beats them for many long days until they discover a means to escape.

When I read that passage as a child, I was amazed that Christian, who had braved fire and water and lions and dragons and darkness and hunger and nakedness and sword, had succumbed to the temptation of something so seemingly trivial as a bit of springy turf underfoot.

But now that I too was a pilgrim, of sorts, I understood.

There comes a time, after walking long distances, day after day, with a heavy pack on your back, when you become preoccupied with your feet. The scenery around you – be it never so beautiful – ceases to engage you.

If the way is stony, as much of the route between Drumnadrochit and Fort Augustus is, you spend your time scrutinizing the ground, looking for patches where the stones are not so large and angular, or for patches of turf springing up through the path, or for anything, in short, that will lessen for a few precious moments the pain in the soles of your feet.

Bunyan, who was a tinker by trade, and therefore well used to walking long distances over rough ground, would have known this, and would have known – as I now do – that, to the tender-footed Pilgrim, a detour along soft meadows is no small temptation.

When we finally arrived, late in the evening, at the village of Fort Augustus, I felt that we had pushed our worn-out bodies too hard. We had taken a pleasant two-day walk and compressed it into a painful one-day slog.

Fort Augustus is home to a dramatic series of locks (gated water-filled enclosures, used to transfer boats between stretches of water at different levels), which connects the southwestern end of Loch Ness to the Caledonian Canal. It's a fine sight, and attracts a lot of tourists. But Wendy and I passed it with barely a glance, and pressed on to the nearby campsite.

The following day's walk was supposed to be an easy ten-miler: first along the towpath of the Caledonian Canal, and then along the banks of Loch Oich to a free camping site at Laggan Locks. Unfortunately, the weather was foul. So what should have been a gentle stroll turned out to be a wet and windy tramp.

I enjoyed it though. Partly because it was nice and short, which meant that I had plenty of free time to look forward to at the end of the day. And partly because this section of the Caledonian Canal is so very interesting.

Before setting out on the Great Glen Way, I had assumed that the Caledonian Canal would be like every other canal I've ever walked along: a narrow waterway populated by cute little barges.

But it isn't.

The Caledonian Canal is actually a shipping lane that runs the entire length of the Great Glen, enabling boats of considerable size to navigate their way across country from the northeast coast to the southwest coast of Scotland.

It was designed and built by Thomas Telford during the first half of the nineteenth century, and consists of twenty-two miles of man-made canal connecting thirty-eight miles of loch. Along its route there are three lochs, twenty-nine locks, ten bridges, and four aqueducts.

Work on the Caledonian Canal began at the turn of the century when the sailing ship was still king. But, by the time it was completed, steam-powered ships ruled the waves. Many of these were too large to navigate the canal, which meant that it was a commercial failure. It soon began to establish itself as a tourist attraction, however, and now attracts hundreds of thousands of visitors each year.

On a map, the Caledonian Canal looks like an enormous zip-fastener running between the northern and southern parts of the Scottish mainland. In fact, it seems to me that, were it not for the twenty-nine locks stapling the two land masses together, the northern part would effectively be a separate island.

The Caledonian Canal, then, is not your average canal. So, although my feet were still sore, and although the wind and rain were driving into my face for much of the day, I enjoyed watching the numerous pleasure boats scooting along the canal, navigating the locks, and zipping along the expansive waters of Loch Oich.

The weather was so foul that day that we abandoned our plans to camp at Laggan Locks, and instead plumped for the relative comfort of a private room at the Great Glen Hostel, in the tiny hamlet of **South Laggan**.

We arrived early in the afternoon, which gave us heaps of time to hang our wet things in the drying room, to shower, to cook dinner, to eat and drink, and to relax. This early finish to the day, along with the unaccustomed luxury of a night in a hostel, was a tonic to my weary soul. I felt that, if every day were like this, JoGLE might be a very jolly affair.

Our room was small and simply furnished. It had a bunk-bed, a chair, a desk, and a radiator. And it was heaven.

For two weeks, Wendy and I had stayed in a backpacker tent that was too small to allow us to sit upright. Night after night, we had squeezed ourselves into sleeping-bags, lay down on three-quarter-length inflatable mattresses, propped up our feet on loose piles of clothing, and rested our heads on travel pillows.

But, here, we had a comfortable room, a carpet to stand on, a chair to sit on, and proper mattresses to lie on.

The hostel itself had a kitchen, a dining area, and a lounge. And this too was heaven.

For two weeks, we had cooked our meals on a one-ring burner, sat cross-legged on the floor to eat, and chased the food around our plates using a plastic 'spork' (a combination fork/spoon).

But, here, we had a multi-ring hob, a table, chairs, and proper cutlery.

Last, but by no means least, the hostel had towels for hire.

For two weeks, we'd 'dried' ourselves, after showering, using travel towels: small, leathery items that push water around the body rather than removing it.

But, here, for a small fee, we were able to dry ourselves with proper fluffy towels.

Suddenly, the most basic comforts, which we had taken for granted all our lives, took on the character of splendid luxuries.

After a glorious night's sleep, and a glorious breakfast of cereal *and toast*, Wendy and I set off on a modest thirteen-mile hike along the western shore of Loch Lochy to **Gairlochy**.

Our route lay mostly along forest tracks, which are generally rather dull work. But not on this day.

The previous evening, I had introduced Wendy to an idea that had been brewing in my mind for a day or two. The idea of 'Gary-time'.

Gary-time was my proposed solution to two separate problems. The first was that I was finding long-distance walking rather too monotonous, and needed to inject some mental stimulation into my routine if I were to reach Land's End psychologically intact. The second was that constant companionship – even Wendy's – was becoming too much for a dyed-in-the-wool introvert like me, and I needed to get some regular doses of mental space if I were to avoid frustration and grumpiness.

My proposed solution to both problems was that each day I would spend some walking time listening to audio-books or music on my smartphone. This would provide me with both the mental stimulation and the uninterrupted periods of solitude I required.

I confess to having had some misgivings about broaching the subject with Wendy. I thought that perhaps she would find the concept of Gary-time offensive. But, in fact, she was cool with it. Perhaps – and this thought has only just occurred to me – she was glad of the opportunity to enjoy some Wendy-time.

So, that day, I enlivened a two-hour stretch of the forest path between South Laggan and Gairlochy by listening to the audiobook *Buddhism for Beginners*, by the American Buddhist teacher and author Jack Kornfield.

At one point, Kornfield shared a poem by the seventeenth-century Japanese monk Gensei.

Gensei describes taking an autumn walk, coming to a stream, and finding that the bridge across it has been washed away by the rain. Undeterred, he removes his sandals and wades through, delighting in the shallowness of the stream and the firmness of the rocks beneath his feet.

The poem ends:

> *The point in life is to know what's enough –*
> *why envy those otherworld immortals?*
> *With the happiness held in one inch-square heart*
> *you can fill the whole space between heaven and earth.*

The poem conjured up some nice images. Even so, I would normally have passed over it without much thought, and perhaps soon forgotten it. But not on this day. On this day, I felt a deep connection with the poet and his state of mind.

In the same way that he had delighted in the shallowness of the stream and the firmness of the rocks, I too had begun to appreciate the familiar qualities of everyday objects: the soft absorbency of a towel, the firm supportiveness of a chair, the warmth and comfort of a carpeted floor.

I had experienced those things every day for almost half a century. Yet I had never really attended to them, and never really appreciated them. I had never realized that everyday life holds such an abundance of simple pleasures.

I wondered if it would be possible for me to hold onto that realization when JoGLE was over; when towels and chairs and tables and beds became commonplace again.

It occurred to me that the man or woman who, like Gensei, could hold onto that realization, and could take ever-fresh delight in the simple pleasures of life, would require few possessions to be richer than Croesus.

These interesting and pleasant thoughts occupied my mind as I walked through the forests on the western shore of Loch Lochy. At other times, when the path emerged from the trees, the view of the loch and the towering mountains in the distance was enough.

At lunchtime, Wendy and I took advantage of a spell of sunshine and stopped for a picnic on a rocky shore. I can still see her, sitting there, on a rock beneath a bent old tree, in her red wind-shirt and battered sun-hat, with her rucksack at her feet, looking for all the world like the jolly swagman who sat by a billabong under the shade of a coolibah tree.

Our destination was Gairlochy, which consists of little more than two pretty locks, which connect a section of the Caledonian Canal to the southern end of Loch Lochy.

We arrived there quite early in the afternoon. However, the nearest campsite was a mile or two off the trail, which meant that we had to finish an otherwise pleasant day with some tedious and unproductive road-walking.

We had passed no shops that day. Nor on the previous day. So we decided to use our emergency packets of dehydrated potatoes and meatballs for dinner. We'd bought them prior to setting off on JoGLE, and had been carrying them for the best part of two hundred miles.

They were horrible.

The following morning, we feasted – in the loosest sense of the word – on cereal bars before retracing our steps to Gairlochy, ready for our final assault on the Great Glen Way.

We had just twelve miles to cover. And because they were flat, easy miles, and because the sun was shining, and because, after two consecutive days of short walks, our feet were feeling a whole lot better, we felt good.

First, we walked along a pretty section of towpath that runs between the canal and the River Lochy, arriving around lunchtime at Neptune's Staircase, a magnificent series of eight individual locks, which joins the Caledonian Canal with the sea loch, Loch Linnhe, sixty-four feet below.

From there, our route ran alongside Loch Linnhe, with fine

views of Ben Nevis, Britain's highest mountain, then through a housing estate in the village of Corpach, and finally into **Fort William**, the largest town in the West Highlands.

Our destination was the Glen Nevis Caravan and Camping Park, an enormous campsite catering for the vast numbers of campers, caravanners, hikers, climbers, mountain-bikers, cyclists, and other assorted nature enthusiasts that converge upon Fort William each year.

To get there, we had to walk through the town centre, past the obelisk that marks the southern end of the Great Glen Way, and then past the signpost that marks the northern end of the West Highland Way. So, in a single day, we got to finish one national walking trail and begin another.

The campsite was beautifully situated in a deep valley at the foot of the mighty Ben Nevis. The afternoon was young. We had the entire evening ahead of us, and an entire day off to look forward to. Life was good.

One thing I learned very quickly on JoGLE is the inestimable value of a day off.

A day off provides you with necessary rest for your tender feet and tired body. It relieves you of the morning chore of taking down your tent and the evening chore of setting it up again. It gives you time to wash and dry your clothes, to stock up on groceries, to plan the next stage of your journey, and even to lounge around reading a novel or listening to music.

It's an oasis of ease and comfort.

To the non-walker, it may sound strange to hear a day spent camping in a backpacker tent, catching up on laundry, and shopping for groceries described as an oasis of ease and comfort.

But comfort is a relative concept.

Georg Wilhelm Friedrich Hegel, the nineteenth-century German philosopher, wrote: 'What the English call "comfort" is something inexhaustible and illimitable. Others can reveal to you that what you take to be comfort at any stage is discomfort, and these discoveries never come to an end.'

He was absolutely right.

For example, when you sleep every night in a backpacker tent, your idea of comfort is a hostel bed, a proper cooker, and a table and chairs. When you sleep every night in a hostel, your idea of comfort is your own little house with its own little kitchen, bedroom, and bathroom. When you live in your own little house, your idea of comfort is a big house with a designer kitchen, more en-suite bedrooms than you know what to do with, and a double garage.

And even when you have all of that, you still find yourself hankering after further comforts: better TVs, faster broadband, reclining armchairs, plusher carpets . . .

However much you have, you will always want more.

This insatiable hunger for ever-greater levels of comfort is fuelled, in large part, says Hegel, by 'others', by the people around you who have bigger, better, nicer stuff than you do, and by the advertisers whose mission in life is to convince you that nobody in their right mind could possibly be content with the stuff you have right now.

Epicurus understood that. That's why he and his disciples moved outside the city, away from 'others' and out of temptation's way.

Epicurus also understood that you pay for your comforts. And not just with money. You pay for them with long hours at the office, work-related stress, frenetic family life, and lack of time and energy for the things that really interest you.

Far better, he argued, to learn to be content with what is sufficient rather than to be constantly striving for more. 'Nothing is enough for the man to whom enough is too little,' he said.

Or, as Gensei put it, 'The point in life is to know what's enough.'

If one keeps on walking, everything will be alright.

———

—KIERKEGAARD, *LETTER TO HENRIETTA*

CHAPTER THREE

Open Spaces

*Fort William – Kinlochleven – King's House
Hotel – Tyndrum – Inverarnan – Rowardennan –
Drymen – Milngavie*

THE ROAD BETWEEN JOHN O'GROATS AND INVERNESS IS almost unremittingly dull. The Great Glen Way, like the curate's egg, is good in parts. But the West Highland Way is sublime.

It runs ninety-six miles from Fort William to Milngavie, near Glasgow, through some of the wildest, remotest, and loveliest parts of the Scottish Highlands. It meanders through pastoral landscapes, passes between rugged peaks, stretches across desolate moors, cuts through leafy forests, and runs beside serene lochs.

It attracts seventy-five thousand visitors a year, of which thirty thousand walk the entire trail. But you'd never know it. You pass other walkers now and then, but in the main you have the mountains, the moors, the forests, and the lochs to yourself.

Our first day's walk on the West Highland Way took us thirteen miles from **Fort William** to **Kinlochleven**, a none-too-pretty village, prettily situated on the eastern side of Loch Leven, and surrounded on three sides by mountains.

An hour or so into the morning, on a long ascent through a forest at the edge of Glen Nevis, we saw two young men limping towards us. I mean, *really* limping – worse, even, than Wendy when she had limped into Dunbeath.

They hobbled up alongside us, tight-lipped and wincing with pain, and asked, 'How much further?'

It turned out that they had walked almost the entire length of the West Highland Way, going from south to north, in just four days, and were about to complete the last few miles after wild-camping nearby on the previous night.

They were young and strong, and had been confident that they could cope with the punishing schedule they had set for themselves. But they had reckoned without the blisters.

They *all* reckon without the blisters.

Just three weeks previously, Wendy and I had reckoned without the blisters. But now, with 120 miles of road and 70 miles of walking trail behind us, we knew better.

We assured them that they hadn't far to go, and that their trials would soon be over. But, in truth, I felt sure that their trashed feet would continue to hurt them for a long time yet.

After wishing them well, we resumed our journey: out of the forest, along an old military road through an empty glen, and then down a wooded hillside to our campsite in Kinlochleven.

It was on this day that I began to think of myself, for the first time, as a walker.

I had now hiked almost two hundred miles, carrying a heavy rucksack up and down hills, through sun and rain, along highways and byways, through towns and villages, and through forests and moors and glens. And I still had a thousand miles to go.

I had endured fatigue, blisters, aches and pains, sunburn, and boredom. Yet I was still going. And I was going stronger than ever.

In the early days of JoGLE, I had always found the last few miles of each day to be a dull, painful slog. But now I found them merely dull. The pain wasn't there any more. Or, if it was, I had become inured to it.

Also, in the early days, I had found my rucksack to be a cumbersome, wearisome, and thoroughly loathsome object. It had seemed terribly heavy back then. Whenever I stopped for a break, I would put it down with a feeling of exquisite relief. And when the break was over I would have to steel myself to the task of taking it up again.

But now my rucksack felt like part of me. And, although it still felt heavy at times, at other times I would walk for miles barely conscious of it.

As a long-distance walker, I had gone from zero to hero, from bumbling novice to seasoned pro, in just a few short weeks.

On the following day, Wendy and I had planned to walk twenty-one miles from Kinlochleven to the tiny village of Bridge of Orchy. But, with heavy rain forecast, we decided that discretion was the better part of valour, and opted instead to walk just nine miles to a popular wild-camping site beside the **King's House Hotel**.

This short section of the West Highland Way is a straight-forward up-and-down affair: up the Devil's Staircase, a zigzag track ascending the rocky ridge of Aonach Eagach, and then back down again.

Wendy, inspired by the dramatic views of the Glencoe Mountains and stimulated by the physical challenge of the Devil's Staircase, was in tremendous form, and spent the day striding forward with great gusto. I, on the other hand, felt unaccountably lacklustre, and spent the day lagging behind.

Even heroes and seasoned pros, it seems, have their off days.

That afternoon, just before the rain began, we pitched our tent, as best we could, amidst a scattering of other tents and a few billion midges on the scrubby moorland at the back of the King's House Hotel. Then we headed into the hotel's Climbers' Bar and stayed there, out of reach of the rain and the midges, until closing time.

The King's House Hotel is reputed to be one of Scotland's oldest licensed inns, and is certainly one of its most remote. It was built in the seventeenth century to cater for travellers crossing nearby Rannoch Moor, and now caters for fisherman, hikers, climbers, and skiers.

Those with sufficient funds can retire to one of the hotel's bedrooms, after closing time, and can look out of their picture windows upon the mountains, the moors, the wind, the rain, and the deer. But Wendy and I, being without sufficient funds, had to retire to our backpacker tent and keep more intimate company with the mountains, the moors, the wind, the rain, and the midges.

Midges are mosquito-like biting insects that infest large parts of the Highlands and Western Scotland during the summer months. They're so tiny that they're barely visible to the human eye, but there are *lots* of them. A square metre of ground can hold *half a million*. So it's little consolation to know that only the females bite.

Each summer, midges ruin countless picnics, walks, and camping trips. They make thousands of visitors vow never to set foot in the Scottish countryside again, and are estimated to cost the tourist industry £300 million a year.

Despite taking every precaution to prevent midges from entering our inner tent in the night, Wendy and I woke up the next morning covered in itchy lumps. Then, when we ventured outside, we were descended upon by hordes of the little bastards.

One midge bite is no big deal. It feels like a tiny, hot pinprick. But a full-scale attack, consisting of perhaps a dozen hot pinpricks per second, drives you to distraction. So we dived back into the tent and covered every square inch of skin with long-trousers, long-sleeved shirts, gloves, and mesh hoods. Only then could we take down our camp, ready to set off on the

day's hike: nineteen miles from the King's House Hotel to
Tyndrum, including a lengthy stretch across Rannoch Moor.

Rannoch Moor is a vast wilderness of peat bogs, streams, lochs,
and lochans, a fifty-square-mile elevated plateau encircled by
mountains.

In Robert Louis Stevenson's *Kidnapped*, the narrator, David
Balfour, says of Rannoch Moor, 'A wearier-looking desert never
man saw'. But he was fleeing for his life and dangerously ill at
the time. So doubtlessly that coloured his perceptions.

My experience of it was very different. I found it to be a wild
and lovely place. Something about it – something to do with its
vastness and openness, and its harsh, untamed beauty – seemed
to set my soul free.

Generally, in my everyday life, my thoughts writhe and
churn inside my head like the proverbial can of worms. But
there, on the moor, they seemed to find release. I felt smaller
than I usually do, and less important than I usually do, and it
was a good feeling.

I recalled that I had felt the same way twenty years previously
while walking in the Lake District. I was in my early thirties at
the time, and undergoing a crisis of faith.

I had grown up believing that there is a God and a Devil,
that Christians go to Heaven while everyone else goes to Hell,

that the Bible is right about *everything*, and that one day – probably very soon – Jesus will come again.

Needless to say, I had the occasional pang of doubt about all of this. But up until my late twenties I managed to keep on believing nonetheless. However, as my twenties gave way to my thirties, I found that my doubts had become too big to brush under the carpet any more. I had to face them.

If I could resolve my doubts – and I sincerely hoped that I could – then I could carry on believing. But otherwise . . .

So it was that I found myself, for the first time, questioning the beliefs that had guided every aspect of my life up until then. It was an intensely stressful and confusing time. I was tied up in so many intellectual and emotional knots that I scarcely knew what – or even how – to think. I felt so burdened and distressed that I wondered if I could ever be happy again.

But, in the middle of it all, I took a fortnight's camping holiday, alone, in the Lake District.

Each day, I would walk through the countryside and allow my thoughts to wander freely. And slowly, surely, and simply, the knots began to unravel. I began to understand who I was and what kind of person I wanted – needed – to become.

Mostly, it was the solitude that helped me to gain clarity. During twenty-odd years in the fundamentalist church, I had acquired a whole host of significant others – pastors, elders, teachers, preachers, house-group leaders, worship leaders, congregation members, friends, and relatives – who all had very strong opinions about who I was and what kind of person I ought to become. With all of their noise and clamour and expectation, I found it impossible to think, or even to feel, for myself. But away from them all, alone in the forests and beside the lakes, I began to discern the beating of my own heart.

Solitude, by itself, though, wouldn't have been enough. It wouldn't have brought me the stillness and clarity that I needed. The walking was important too.

There is something about walking – the steady, unhurried rhythm, the gentle stimulation of heart and lungs, and the pleasant synchronization of mind and body – that soothes the spirit and frees the mind.

This is especially true of walking in the countryside, where the quiet beauty of the surroundings soothes the spirit still further, and where the wide-open spaces offer still greater freedom to the mind.

It was during the second week of that camping trip that I discovered Plato.

One of the things that the solitude and the walking helped me to realize was that I needed to widen my intellectual horizons. I needed to expose myself to some new ideas, and start thinking things through for myself.

So, when I saw a battered old copy of Plato's *Republic* in a second-hand bookshop, I bought it.

I knew nothing about Plato, except that he was an Ancient Greek, and that he was a philosopher. But 'philosopher' meant *thinker* – and that's what I wanted to be.

So I started at page one, and I read the *Republic*.

It wasn't what I expected (though I'm not sure what I *did* expect). It turned out to be a dialogue – a play, of sorts – in which the character Socrates discusses the concept of justice with a bunch of other characters.

It was hard work, and I didn't understand it all. But it excited me anyway, because it exposed me to a whole new way of trying to understand the world.

Socrates and his companions didn't just *tell* each other what to think. They *reasoned* with one another. They *talked*, and they *listened*, and they *thought things through*.

It was the complete opposite of everything I had ever known. And it was brilliant.

For the rest of the week, I carried that battered old copy of the *Republic* with me, and I walked with Plato.

Plato introduced me to philosophy; and philosophy introduced me to Epicurus, Bertrand Russell, William James, Gensei, Hegel, and all of the other great thinkers that have kept me company ever since.

Walking over Rannoch Moor was a joy, but I had little time to savour it. Not so much because the ten-mile crossing of the moor made up only half of the day's journey, leaving plenty of ground still to cover, but rather because the Rannoch midges descended upon us in a feeding frenzy whenever we tried to stop or slow our pace.

Having crossed the moor, we walked for nine miles along the floor of the glen to the Pine Trees Leisure Park in the tourist village of Tyndrum. There, for reasons I can't recall, we splashed out on a 'hiker hut' (a wooden shed, complete with twin beds, electrical sockets, and a kettle) rather than pitching our tent.

The next stage of the West Highland Way, a thirteen-mile jaunt through farmland, forests, and riverside paths, from Tyndrum to **Inverarnan**, passed quickly and pleasantly.

As I walked along, not at all focusing on, but nonetheless enjoying, the varied scenery, I found myself musing on what it is about the countryside that is so soothing to the spirit and so refreshing to the soul. But I couldn't quite put my finger on it. Or, at any rate, I couldn't put it into words.

I felt that it had something to do with the space, with the openness of the fields and the sky. And I felt that it had something to do with the gentle, almost imperceptible, pace at which things change.

Out in the countryside, you're part of something bigger, more important, and longer lasting than yourself. So that you get dwarfed by it all. But in a good way.

The British philosopher and novelist Iris Murdoch expressed it far better than I ever could in her beautiful book *The Sovereignty of Good*:

> I am looking out of my window in an anxious and resent-
> ful state of mind, oblivious of my surroundings, brooding
> perhaps on some damage done to my prestige. Then I
> suddenly observe a hovering kestrel. In a moment

everything is altered. The brooding self with its hurt vanity has disappeared. There is nothing now but kestrel. And when I return to thinking of the other matter it seems less important.

Perhaps all of this explains why so many troubled and depressive thinkers have been avid walkers.

Take the nineteenth-century Danish philosopher Søren Kierkegaard, for example, a man so messed up and brooding and despondent that I consider myself positively cheerful by comparison.

By the age of twenty-one, he had lost his mother and five of his six siblings. He had a religiously melancholic father who viewed these deaths as God's punishment for the sins of his youth. He suffered physical problems, including a curved spine and – quite possibly – sexual impotence.

As a young man, he broke off his engagement to a young woman whom he adored, on the grounds that he could never offer her anything like a normal marriage, and then spent the rest of his life mourning for her loss.

As a child he was ridiculed and bullied by his schoolmates, and as an adult he was ridiculed in the Danish press. To cap all of this, he suffered – perhaps unsurprisingly – from severe and chronic anxiety.

He wrote in his journal: 'The whole of existence makes me anxious, from the smallest fly to the mysteries of the Incarnation. . . . Great is my distress, unlimited.'

At another time he wrote:

> I have just now come from a party where I was its life and
> soul; witticisms streamed from my lips, everyone laughed
> and admired me, but I went away – yes, the dash should
> be as long as the radius of the earth's orbit —————
> and wanted to shoot myself.

This is hard-core depression. Yet even a man afflicted with this level of despair was able to draw comfort and consolation from the simple act of walking.

In 1847, in a letter to his niece Henrietta, he wrote:

> Above all, do not lose your desire to walk; every day I walk
> myself into a state of well-being and walk away from every
> illness. I have walked myself into my best thoughts, and I
> know of no thought so burdensome that one cannot walk
> away from it.

Or, for another example, take the eighteenth-century Genevan philosopher and writer Jean-Jacques Rousseau.

In his old age, at the close of a brilliant, but also a turbulent and unhappy life, he took to walking alone in the countryside around Paris.

A sufferer from poor mental health, Rousseau considered himself to have been the victim of jealousy and persecution throughout his life, and had determined to end his days in withdrawal from the society that he felt had so cruelly mistreated him.

In his final work, *Reveries of a Solitary Walker*, which was unfinished at his death, he describes his walks and the 'flights of thought' that accompanied them. It is a beautiful and lyrical book: sometimes intensely sad and sometimes wonderfully uplifting; sometimes sharply insightful and sometimes narcissistic and paranoid. To me, it paints a picture of a troubled and suspicious man, who, in his solitary walks, finds a measure of tranquillity and contentment that he could find nowhere else.

He writes: 'These hours of solitude and meditation are the only ones in the day during which I am fully myself and for myself, without diversion, without obstacle, and during which I can truly claim to be what nature willed.'

At first glance, neither of these unhappy men seems like a poster boy for the therapeutic power of walking. But my point isn't that countryside walks are a panacea for all forms of depression. It is that depressed people often find it helpful to take country walks.

Mildly depressed people, such as my thirty-year-old self, find that walking helps to put their troubles into perspective and to improve their mood; and more severely depressed people, such as Kierkegaard and Rousseau, find that walking helps to make their lives bearable.

Scientific evidence bears this out. Numerous studies have shown a positive link between walking and mental health.

For example, a study reported in the *British Journal of Sports Medicine* found that walking thirty minutes a day boosted the moods of depressed patients faster than antidepressants. Another study undertaken at California State University, Long Beach, found that the more people walked each day, the more energetic they felt and the better their mood. And a study undertaken by researchers at the University of Stirling revealed that walking had 'a large effect on depression'.

I was fortunate, then, not to be walking for just thirty minutes a day, but to be walking for seven or eight hours a day. And not only that, but also to be walking through some of the wildest, most wide-open, and most inspiring places in Britain.

Small wonder, then, that I was beginning to feel healthier, happier, and more energized than I had felt in a long time.

We stayed for two nights at a busy campsite just outside Inverarnan. It had plenty of facilities, including a sheltered campers' kitchen. But it also had an unloved and uncared-for air about it.

On our second night, as we tried to coax a little heat from a clapped-out electric ring on the clapped-out hob in the kitchen, we fell into conversation with a group of French boys, in their late teens, who were also trying to coax a little heat from a clapped-out ring on the same hob.

They were pleasant boys, who seemed – much to my surprise – to take a genuine interest in the doings of a couple of middle-aged fellow hikers. When they learned that we were walking not just the West Highland Way but the entire length of Britain, they were astonished. One of them nodded approvingly, and then uttered a single word: 'Respect.'

I felt strangely moved.

From Inverarnan, the next stage of our journey took us seven-teen miles to the rural community of **Rowardennan**, much of it along the eastern shore of Loch Lomond.

This has the reputation of being the toughest section of the West Highland Way because the loch-side path, such as it is, constantly rises and falls and requires you to scramble over boulders and pick your way across tree roots.

We had been dreading lugging our backpacks along such difficult terrain, and had anticipated a long, hard day. But, as it turned out, we managed the seventeen miles, and the ups and downs, and the boulders and tree roots quite easily. We had become much leaner, fitter, and tougher than when we started.

Loch Lomond is the largest lake in Great Britain by surface area, and second only to Loch Ness by volume. It is studded with over thirty islands of varying shapes and sizes, and set amidst magnificent mountains, including the magnif-icent Ben Lomond, which lies close to its eastern shore. Consequently, it is considered one of Scotland's finest natu-ral wonders.

Oddly enough, I have only the haziest memories of all of this. What I recall mostly from that day is the wonderful, fully alive, fully engaged feeling I had when scrambling along the loch side, the glorious experience of being totally absorbed in the moment.

Most of the things we do in life, we do for the sake of some-thing else. We work to earn money; we exercise to get fit; we study to pass exams; we watch TV to relax; we engage in spiritual exercises to improve ourselves; and so on.

But life's most sublime moments often occur when we engage in activities entirely for their own sake, without any ulterior motives.

When I was a child, I attended a primary school that had a large oak tree in the middle of its playing field. I recall standing alone, beneath that tree, one crisp autumn afternoon when the leaves were falling slowly but steadily from its branches.

I soon became engrossed in the task of trying to catch those leaves as they fell.

I would look up into the canopy of the tree and wait for a green-brown leaf to come spiralling down. Then I would dodge and dance around, arms outstretched, and try to grab it before it reached the ground.

It was a surprisingly difficult and tremendously absorbing activity. I soon lost all track of time, and lost consciousness of everything except those falling leaves and my desire to catch them. It was an experience of utter mindfulness, in which I achieved a state of near bliss.

I look back on it now as one of my life's most magical experiences. Even today, I sometimes find myself looking wistfully into the canopies of autumn trees.

As I scrambled along the eastern shore of Loch Lomond, moving swiftly over boulders and tree roots, with my heart and lungs working hard, and with my limbs, senses, and mind all working together perfectly, I experienced something of the same exultation: a primitive joy in being alive and healthy, and fully and actively engaged with the natural world.

By four o'clock – much earlier than expected – we had reached our destination, The Shepherd's House B&B, which is situated in a quiet location at the edge of the Rowardennan Forest, on the east shore of Loch Lomond.

We spent the night in a self-contained bedroom-cum-sitting-room-cum-bathroom-on-wheels, modelled on the huts that shepherds once inhabited during lambing season.

Unlike the shepherd's huts of yore, this one was a luxurious and well-appointed affair – though too small to swing a kitten in.

In the morning, breakfast was delivered in a pretty wicker basket, replete with hot and cold eatables and drinkables.

I have a photo of Wendy, perched on the edge of the bed, surveying that hamper and its contents with a look of unalloyed joy. But I don't need the photo to remind me. Her smile is etched into my memory.

There's a quote that is often attributed to the French author and philosopher Albert Camus that goes like this:

> When you have once seen the glow of happiness on the face of a beloved person, you know that a man can have no vocation but to awaken that light on the faces surrounding him; and you are torn by the thought of the unhappiness and night you cast, by the mere fact of living, in the hearts you encounter.

I have my doubts that it was Camus who said it. But, Camus or not, it captures something important and true. The unclouded smile, the 'glow of happiness', on Wendy's face as she surveyed that basket gave me a glorious yet terrifying glimpse of the capacity for happiness within her.

Gensei was right: 'With the happiness held in one inch-square heart you can fill the whole space between heaven and earth.'

The following day's walk took us just eleven miles from Rowardennan to **Drymen** (pronounced *Drimmen*), a village lying a couple of miles east of the southern end of Loch Lomond.

The trail ran first between the loch on our right and the Rowardennan Forest on our left. Then it climbed up and over the sharp little summit of Conic Hill, with splendid views of the loch and its islands. Finally, it meandered through the thick and gloomy Garadhban (pronounced *Garavan*) Forest.

This was another great day for reflection.

In the shepherd's hut, the previous evening, I had been reading Leo Tolstoy's epic novel *War and Peace*, and I was struck by a passage in which one of the book's central characters, Pierre – at this time a prisoner of the retreating French army – is on a forced march of many days' duration across Russia.

At one point, he struggles through heavy rain up a muddy, slippery road. All around him are the carcasses of men and horses in varying stages of decay. He is weak and sick and half-starved and footsore.

As he walks, he counts off his steps on his fingers and mentally addresses the rain: 'Now then, now then, go on! Pelt harder!'

Here, Tolstoy writes: 'It seemed to him that he was thinking of nothing, but far down and deep within him his soul was occupied with something important and comforting.'

Tolstoy doesn't tell us precisely what this 'something' was, merely that it was 'a most subtle spiritual deduction' from a conversation he'd had the day before with his peasant friend and fellow prisoner Karataev. But, whatever it was, it was important and it was comforting.

This passage really struck a chord with me. I felt that I understood precisely what Tolstoy meant.

There's a mode of thinking you get into when you walk long distances that is very deep but largely unconscious. Your mind takes whatever it is that you're currently preoccupied with, or anxious about, or desirous of, or frightened of, and slowly works away at it.

These are things that your conscious mind struggles to deal with because they're too stressful, too abstract, too tied up with your ego, too spiritual, too shameful, too frightening, or too complex. But your unconscious mind works away at them calmly, quietly, and unseen.

Suddenly, you have a burst of inspiration or a flash of insight that feels as though it's come from nowhere. But it hasn't. It's come from deep within you.

As I walked over the hills, across the moors, and through the forests towards Drymen, musing upon the link between walking and inspiration, it occurred to me that some of the people whom I most admire made walking an integral part of their routine.

Charles Dickens was addicted to walking. Often, when working intensely on a project, he would cover fifteen or twenty miles in a single night 'through the black streets of London'.

These brisk, nocturnal walks seemed to act as a physical release for the mental strain and psychological stress of writing. 'If I could not walk far and fast,' he said, 'I think I should just explode and perish.'

But additionally, and just as importantly, walking unleashed his creativity.

He would often plot his novels on the move. *A Christmas Carol*, for example, was brought to birth during a series of nocturnal ramblings in the winter of 1843. He told a friend that he had 'composed it in his head, laughing and weeping and weeping again', as he walked.

Bertrand Russell also incorporated daily walks into his creative routine. Only after spending an hour or two outdoors, pacing around and organizing his thoughts, would he sit down at his desk to write. Then the words flowed quickly and easily from his pen.

Or, to press the point home with just one more example, consider the nineteenth-century German philosopher Friedrich Nietzsche.

Nietzsche suffered bouts of depression throughout his life, which became more prolonged and intense as he grew older, and eventually gave way to madness. (At the time, his mental illness was diagnosed as tertiary syphilis, though it now seems more likely that he was suffering from a slowly developing brain tumour.)

Like Kierkegaard and Rousseau, Nietzsche found walking therapeutic. In fact, his need of it seems to have been even greater than theirs.

For example, during the 1880s, Nietzsche rented a room, most summers, in a house in Sils-Maria, high in the Swiss Alps. While there, health and weather permitting, he would go for two brisk walks each day: a two-hour walk before lunch, and an even longer one after lunch.

These walks, through the forest or along the shores of Lake Silvaplana or Lake Sils, seem to have been necessary for his physical and mental wellbeing. But they were equally necessary for his creativity and inspiration.

As he walked, he would think. And, as thoughts occurred to him, he would jot them down in a notebook. This method of composition gave his philosophy and his writing a very distinctive character. It gave them a boldness and a free-spiritedness that would have been absent had he remained at his desk.

Indeed, Nietzsche went so far as to claim that thinking-while-walking was the *only* way to do philosophy. In his book *Twilight of the Idols*, which he composed in Sils-Maria in the summer of 1888, he wrote: 'A sedentary life is the real sin against the Holy Spirit. Only those thoughts that come by walking have any value.'

In his earlier book *The Gay Science*, he criticized the practice of thinking and writing indoors, hemmed in by narrow walls and low ceilings 'with compressed belly and head bent over paper'. Such surroundings and such a posture, he claimed, can give rise only to stale, constipated thoughts.

He wrote: 'It is our custom to think in the open air, walking, leaping, climbing, or dancing on lonesome mountains by preference, or close to the sea, where even the paths become thoughtful.'

Like Dickens, Russell, and Nietzsche, I too – in my own small way – can testify to the link between walking and creativity.

For me, JoGLE wasn't entirely a holiday. I had very little in the way of work to do, but I did have to produce my 'Living' column for Singapore's national newspaper, *The Straits Times*, once a fortnight.

Generally, I find writing it – or, indeed, writing *anything* – very hard work. I dither about, and suffer crises of confidence, and stare at a blank screen, and go over and over the same few lines without making any actual progress, and generally have a difficult time of it.

But during JoGLE, I wrote more quickly and easily than I have ever written before. I dashed off my column, which normally takes me anything between eight and twelve hours, in just three or four hours – and that while lying in a backpacker tent with no laptop.

The reason was simple. Although I gave no specific thought to my column as I walked, and although I didn't consciously set out to think about anything at all, my mind was constantly turning over thoughts and ideas.

Like Tolstoy's Pierre, my soul was occupied every day with

things 'important and comforting', and so I always had something worthwhile to share.

At Drymen, we camped on a rough-and-ready farm campsite, and then set off, the next morning, on the final section of the West Highland Way.

This was a flat and easy thirteen-mile walk, which took us out of the Highlands, through some rural lowlands and into the centre of **Milngavie** (pronounced *Millguy* or *Mullguy*), a commuter town situated just six miles from Glasgow city centre.

Overall, the walk was very pleasant, as far as I recall. But the thing about it that sticks in my mind is the shock and dismay Wendy and I felt as we entered the outskirts of town and found the footpaths, verges, and bushes littered with cigarette butts, crisp packets, fast-food cartons, and dog-shit.

When you live in a town or a city, you get so used to that stuff that you forget how ugly and depressing and dehumanizing it all is. But after spending a few weeks on the moors, in the glens, and beside the lochs and streams, you see it all afresh – and it disgusts you.

We dutifully visited the obelisk that marks the southern end of the West Highland Way, which is incongruously situated on a pedestrianized street in the town centre, and then shopped for supplies, before heading a mile or so out of town to our campsite at Bankell Farm.

That night, just before sleep, a strange and unexpected thought entered my head.

Up to that point, during four weeks of JoGLE, I'd always thought of our backpacker tent as nothing more than a necessary inconvenience.

Necessary, because backpacking is the only way to do End to End without breaking the bank. Over the course of three months, camping works out approximately £5,000 cheaper than B&B-ing.

Inconvenient, because the tent has to be lugged around for eight hours a day, because it has to be erected each evening and taken down each morning, because it isn't big enough to hold you and your stuff comfortably, because it's wet through with dew every morning when you have to pack it away, and because it's infuriatingly difficult to get out of and back into when you need the loo in the night.

So, bearing all of this in mind, it came as a surprise, as I drifted off to sleep that final night on the West Highland Way, to find the thought 'I love my tent!' popping unannounced into my head.

Whether it was the expression of a genuine emotion or the product of some half-sleeping delirium, I couldn't – and still can't – say.

But what if man had eyes to see the true beauty –
the divine beauty, I mean, pure and clear and
unalloyed, not clogged with the pollutions
of mortality and all the colours and vanities
of human life – thither looking, and holding
converse with the true beauty, simple and divine?

—PLATO, *SYMPOSIUM*

CHAPTER FOUR

Sentimental Journey

Milngavie – Falkirk – Linlithgow –
Kirknewton – Carlops – Innerleithen –
Melrose – Jedburgh – Byrness

BEFORE SETTING OUT ON JOGLE, WENDY AND I SPENT A long time pondering how to get from the end of the West Highland Way, at Milngavie, to the start of the Pennine Way, at Kirk Yetholm. There's no established walking route between these two places. There are few campsites and fewer hostels. And there's not much in the way of scenery either.

In the end, we decided to enliven the journey by taking an indirect route via Edinburgh, the Scottish capital, which we both adore. Apart from that, we had low expectations for this part of the journey. And, in the main, our expectations were fulfilled. Looking back, there are entire days I struggle to remember.

But, although the outer journey was dull, the inner journey wasn't. Thoughts and ideas bloomed in those unstimulating surroundings like flowers in the desert.

We began with a twenty-four-mile forced march from **Milngavie** to **Falkirk**, most of it along the towpath of the Forth and Clyde Canal. Rain was forecast, so we decided to leave our tent at Milngavie, walk without backpacks, and return to Milngavie by train at the end of the day.

The Forth and Clyde Canal isn't Britain's prettiest waterway. It's wide and quiet, and has an excellent towpath, but the view is often obscured by trees. And even when there *is* a view, it is often of nothing more inspiring than industrial parks and housing estates.

The route has one highlight though, namely the Falkirk Wheel, the world's only rotating boat lift. This 114-feet-high landmark structure, which connects the Forth and Clyde Canal to the Union Canal, manages to be both a magnificent piece of engineering and a breath-taking modern sculpture at the same time.

Apparently, the design took its inspiration from, among other things, a Celtic axe, the ribcage of a whale, and the propeller of a ship, but to me it resembles nothing so much as a giant corkscrew. In any case, it's a splendid sight, which attracts half a million visitors a year.

Of course, Wendy and I weren't so much visiting the Wheel as marching past it. We didn't reach it until late in the afternoon, and had to press on for two more miles before we reached Falkirk High railway station.

On our journey back to Milngavie, we shared a train with a crowd of business-suited Glasgow commuters. It felt strange, after a month of solitary tramping through the countryside, to be back in mainstream society, and I felt a little sorry for all of those people with their briefcases, laptops, and mobile phones.

That day's walk was the longest so far: a total of twenty-eight miles, including the walk to and from Milngavie Station. It hadn't been the most exciting of walks either. But, despite its length and lack of stimulation, it wasn't unpleasant.

On the very first stage of JoGLE, between John o'Groats and Inverness, I had found the last few miles of each day dull and painful. By the third stage, on the West Highland Way, I had ceased to find them painful, and found them merely dull. And by this fourth stage, even the dullness had ceased to be an issue.

Don't get me wrong. The dullness was still there, to a degree. It just wasn't a big deal any more. I had adjusted to it. Accepted it. Even begun to embrace it.

Each day had a predictable rhythm: a mildly tedious start to the morning with the quotidian chore of taking down our camp. Then five or six hours of enjoyable walking with energy levels high. Then an hour's weary plodding, late in the afternoon. And finally, a congenial evening of food, rest, and relaxation.

And it was a *nice* rhythm, consisting of modest highs and lows that flowed seamlessly from one to another like the peaks and troughs of a sine wave. It had a balance about it, and a tranquillity about it. The modest lows offset the modest highs, and the modest highs offset the modest lows. So, in a curious way, it was all good.

In *The Conquest of Happiness*, Bertrand Russell suggests that too much excitement may not be a good thing, and that a certain amount of boredom may be a necessary ingredient of a happy life:

There is an element of boredom which is inseparable from the avoidance of too much excitement, and too much excitement not only undermines the health, but dulls the palate for every kind of pleasure, substituting titillations for profound organic satisfactions, cleverness for wisdom, and jagged surprises for beauty.

By this stage of JoGLE, I had begun to appreciate what he meant.

Many of us, nowadays, feel compelled to fill every waking moment of our lives with TV, music, Facebook, text messages, tweets, and smartphone apps. We can't abide the thought of sitting quietly, even for a moment, with our thoughts. We crave excitement and stimulation, and regard boredom with abhorrence and fear.

But long-distance walking changed all of that for me. It taught me that periods of mild boredom are nothing to be afraid of. In fact, they can be a good thing.

On a typical day, I walked for about eight hours. I spent perhaps an hour or two of this listening to music and audiobooks, and perhaps an hour or two conversing with Wendy. This left me with at least four hours in which I had nothing to do but walk and think.

Those quiet hours, free from electronic stimuli, and free from talk, work, and play, were sometimes a little dull. And in the early stages that dullness worried and bothered me. But, as time went by, the worry and the bother faded. I came to regard periods of mild boredom not as an enemy but as a companion – and even as a friend.

Those long, empty hours were a cold-turkey cure for my addiction to stimulation and distraction. And, although the cure was painful at first, once it had taken effect, I felt liberated. My mind acquired a newfound tranquillity, clarity, and focus.

The following morning, we packed up our tent, hoisted up our backpacks, walked to the railway station, caught the train back to Falkirk, and then walked ten miles along the Union Canal to **Linlithgow**.

I remember little about the walk except that the Union Canal was much prettier than the Forth and Clyde Canal, and that Wendy suffered a couple of hours of agony after being bitten on the inside of her lip by an insect.

Linlithgow boasts the magnificent ruins of a royal palace, a beautiful little loch, a fine medieval church, and a high street replete with historic buildings. However, all of this passed me by unnoticed. I recall getting my hair cut by a barber who removed my ear hair by setting fire to it, and I recall eating fish and chips out of a box, and that's about it.

But, although I have forgotten the day's sights, I remember very clearly the music I listened to as I walked. With only a week left in Scotland, I had opted for some traditional Scottish songs. And they really got to me.

In the past, I've observed a tendency in myself, when I'm worn out or stressed or depressed, to become emotional at the drop of a hat. I've found myself moved to tears by such unlikely stimuli as advertisements for Sunny Delight and episodes of *Bargain Hunt*.

On this day, though, I felt neither worn out nor stressed nor depressed, and yet I found myself welling up at the words to songs. For example, these lines from 'When You and I were Young, Maggie':

> *They say we are agèd and grey, Maggie,*
> *As spray by the white breakers flung,*
> *But to me you're as fair as you were, Maggie,*
> *When you and I were young.*

Or these words from 'The Road and the Miles to Dundee':

> *I took the gowd pin, from the scarf on my bosom,*
> *And said 'keep ye this, in re-mem-brance O' me',*
> *Then brave-ly I kissed, the sweet lips O' the lassie*
> *E'er I part-ed wi' her, On the road to Dundee.*

I was surprised to find myself in such a tearfully sentimental mood in the absence of any of the usual triggers.

Don't get me wrong, I've always been partial to a bit of senti-mentality – which explains, in part, my adoration of Dickens. But by this stage of JoGLE, I seemed to have got into an unusu-ally heightened state. My feelings – all of them – had become more intense.

Walking for hours each day, attuned to the rhythms of my own breath, heartbeat, and footfall, and with a mind free of distraction and stimulation, had put me into a meditative state.

And, like many a meditator before me, I achieved a higher level of consciousness. I began to *think* more clearly, to *feel* more intensely, to *understand* more deeply, and to *appreciate* more fully.

This enabled me to enter right into the words, music, and sentiments of those wonderful old songs: one moment striding along, arms swinging, bellowing out the words to 'Loch Lomond', and the next moment getting misty-eyed over the bittersweet parting on the 'Road to Dundee'.

I don't recall the sixteen-mile walk from Linlithgow to **Kirknewton**. I imagine that we took an indirect route along the towpath of the Union Canal (looking at the map that would seem the obvious thing to do). But it's possible that we took some other route.

What I *do* remember is looking at Wendy, as we walked the last half-mile into Kirknewton, and being surprised at how exhausted she looked. I, on the other hand, felt as fresh as a daisy and as strong as an ox.

This was such a role reversal, Wendy being the *walker*, that I couldn't resist posting on Facebook, 'New walking-partner required. I've worn the old one out.'

This was met with incredulity and outrage among Wendy's friends. 'I don't believe it! Wendy would *never* give up!' being a typical response. So, for a brief time, I got to experience the perverse thrill of Internet trolling.

Kirknewton is a village situated just southwest of Edinburgh, which has, as far as I know, nothing to recommend it to visitors.

Our only purpose in going there was to catch a train to Edinburgh where we had arranged to spend a couple of nights with our friends Marilyn and Raphie.

Wendy and I had spent two years living in Edinburgh, and it's our favourite place in the world. So we had a splendid time there, visiting old haunts and enjoying our friends' open-hearted hospitality. On the second evening, we even managed to squeeze in a visit to the cinema and eat dinner at a proper restaurant – just like regular people.

From Edinburgh, we took the train back to Kirknewton, and then set off on a five-day hike southeast to Kirk Yetholm.

We'd intended to break up the journey wherever we could find cheap accommodation. But cheap accommodation is in short supply in that part of Scotland. Consequently, for our first night, we had to book an expensive (by our standards) room at a pub-hotel in the village of **Carlops**.

The ten-mile walk to Carlops took us across the Pentland Hills, which lie southwest of Edinburgh. It was a pleasant stroll through upland pastures and heather-clad moors. And, although we were never more than ten miles from the city centre, the hills were so empty and quiet that we might have been a hundred miles from anywhere.

On such a short, easy walk, there was no point hurrying. So we spent the day ambling rather than hiking, and stopped frequently to enjoy the scenery. I spent a lot of time listening to music as I walked, and supplemented traditional Scottish songs with rock-and-roll hits of the fifties and sixties. It was fabulous.

Walking, and having nothing to do except walk, and having nothing to distract me and pull me out of the moment as I walked, enabled me to listen to music the way I listened to it as a teenager: with complete and unforced attention.

Certain songs moved me deeply, especially, I noticed, those that expressed simple heartfelt emotions. For example, The Teddy Bears' 1958 hit 'To Know Him is to Love Him', The Dixie Cups' 1964 hit 'Chapel of Love', and the 1964 hit 'Soldier Boy' by The Shirelles.

Those songs rekindled the feeling I had when I was in my late teens and suddenly realized that life and happiness were simple matters after all: love this girl . . . win this girl . . . and, in the words of The Dixie Cups, 'never be lonely any more'.

This is the essence of romantic love, which Schopenhauer describes so accurately and so pithily as 'this longing that closely associates the notion of an endless bliss with the possession of a definite woman, and an unutterable pain with the thought that this possession is not available'.

Most of us have felt like this at some period of our lives. And few of us have not since learned that life and love are never quite so simple. But those sentimental old songs with their naive optimism take us back to those wonderful times – which is, I guess, why we love them so much.

And the interesting thing about them, artistically speaking, is the emotional punch they pack into a few simple words.

It doesn't take a genius, of course, to understand that simple words can be an effective medium for expressing uncomplicated emotions. But knowing precisely which words to use, and in what order to put them – that's the tricky bit. That's where the artistry comes in.

Take some of those early Beatles songs for example: 'Love me Do', 'Ask Me Why', 'From Me to You', and so on. They use simple words to express uncomplicated emotions, but, even though they're great songs, they pack no emotional punch. It's hard to imagine anyone ever getting misty-eyed over 'Love Me Do'.

Now, by way of contrast, consider 'To Know Him is to Love Him'.

The first verse uses just fourteen different words, thirteen of them polysyllabic, but it captures perfectly – and I mean *perfectly* – the tenderness and innocence of early-stage romantic love.

So what's so special about *those* words in *that* order? And how does the songwriter choose them?

I spent a long time, as I ambled across the Pentland Hills, musing upon this. When, for example, Phil Spector wrote the magical first line of 'To Know Him is to Love Him' was it poetic inspiration? Or did he just get lucky?

Ditto for the equally simple-yet-poignant lyrics of 'Chapel of Love' and 'Soldier Boy'. Did the songwriters lovingly craft those words, knowing that they perfectly express the excitement and unalloyed joy of young love? Or did they just stumble upon them?

In my normal, distracted, overstimulated frame of mind, I don't suppose I would have made much progress on those questions. But in my walking-induced, meditative frame of mind, I felt that I had the time, the energy, and the clarity of mind to pursue them.

I came to the conclusion that moments of perfection in song-writing occur when the artist is completely attuned with both subject and medium.

When I say that the songwriter must be attuned with her subject, I mean that she must have a profound insight into the aspect of experience that she wants to share. There's a parallel, here, with *kado*, the Japanese art of flower-arranging.

In his splendid book *The Japanese Way of the Artist*, the calligrapher and martial-artist H.E. Davey says of the kado-practitioner: 'If she perceives the rhythm and alternation of the *ki* [life-force] of plants and blossoms – their growth, decline and death, how they change in form and feeling with the seasons – then she can successfully arrange flowers.'

And that's precisely how it is with the songwriter. If she's attuned to the rhythm and alternation of the *ki*, the life-force, of romantic love – its growth, decline, and death, and how it changes in form and feeling with the seasons – then she can successfully write a love song.

The song may ostensibly be about just one phase of love, perhaps its beginning or its end. But in the listener it will awaken thoughts and feelings about love's entire course.

This means that a truly great song about the joy and inno-cence of early-stage love will evoke subtle feelings of sadness for love's decline, and a truly great song about the heartbreak of declining love will evoke subtle feelings of joy for love's arising.

When I say that the artist must be attuned with her medium, I mean that she must be skilled in using the tools and techniques of her craft.

Again, in *The Japanese Way of the Artist*, Davey recounts how he once watched his *shodo* [Japanese calligraphy] teacher execute, many times, without the slightest hesitation, a beautiful and evocative brush-stroke. He says, 'To a casual observer it might have seemed to be nothing more than a quick flick of the brush; but to me, someone who had many times tried to produce this particular and powerful brush stroke, it was much more.'

Similarly, when a songwriter creates a lyrical and musical phrase that perfectly captures some aspect of experience, it may appear nothing to the casual observer. But to me, someone who has tried many times to capture the essence of a thought, an idea, or an experience in words, it's much more. It's a triumph of craft, experience, and skill.

The first verse of The Shirelles' 'Soldier Boy' is a prime example. They're just a few simple brush-strokes, but they're perfectly executed. They make no attempt to *describe* the naive ecstasy of young love, but they *suggest* it. They awaken many thoughts and feelings – sad as well as sweet.

And just as you could look for hours at a piece of Japanese calligraphy – perhaps a single *kanji* executed from a few swift brush-strokes – and find nothing in it that could be improved, so you could sit for hours and ponder those lyrics, and find not a syllable that could be altered for the better.

And then, of course, there's the music. Without it, the lyrics of most pop songs are sterile. Silly even.

So what's the magic of music? What gives certain sequences of notes (mere vibrations in the air) the power to bring words to life, and to move us so deeply?

That's quite a question.

I remember, as a child, waking up one summer morning to the sound of music.

I shared a bedroom wall with the little girl next door. She'd received a Bontempi organ for her birthday, and was practising her first tune, the opening to 'Morning Mood' from Grieg's *Peer Gynt Suite*.

For a long time, I lay in bed listening as she repeated the same notes over and over and over again: C-A-G-F-GA C-A-G-F-GAGA . . . (pause) . . . C-A-G-F-GA C-A-G-F-GAGA.

It was the loveliest thing I'd ever heard.

I knew nothing about classical music. I'd never heard of Grieg, and wouldn't have known *Peer Gynt* from *Carmen*. But those notes, badly played, with one finger, on a child's plastic instrument, filled me with an exquisite longing that I'd never known before.

I didn't realize it then, but it was my first encounter with Beauty.

When the music stopped, I lay puzzling over what had happened. Those notes had set me longing for something. Something other-worldly. Something intangible. But what?

Little did I realize that, forty-odd years later, I'd still be grappling with the same question.

Plato grappled with it too.

Plato is probably the greatest, most influential philosopher ever to have lived. In fact, the twentieth-century English philosopher Alfred North Whitehead once summed up the entire European philosophical tradition as 'a series of footnotes to Plato'.

Clearly, then, Plato had a lot of important and interesting stuff to say about a lot of important and interesting stuff. But, for my money, the most important and interesting stuff he ever said was about Beauty.

He too had encountered Beauty, in its various guises, and he too struggled – though admittedly with more success than me – to understand it.

One of his early dialogues, *Hippias Major*, is entirely devoted to the question 'What is Beauty?' In it, two characters, Socrates and Hippias, thrash out the question together, and come up with six increasingly sophisticated attempted definitions, beginning with 'a beautiful maiden is beautiful' and ending with 'the beautiful is that which is pleasing through hearing and sight'. But none of these definitions proves satisfactory. None of them gets to the heart of what Beauty is.

Plato continued to wrestle with the same question throughout his life, and came up with ever more sophisticated – and, some would say, ever more fanciful – answers.

Eventually, he decided that, in addition to all of the individual beautiful things in the world – all of the beautiful faces, flowers, sunsets, landscapes, poems, and melodies – there had to be something more. There had to be Beauty Itself.

Beauty Itself is divine. It is perfect and eternal. It exists outside the physical world, beyond space and time. It is the source of all earthly beauty, and of all that is good and right and true. It is invisible to the senses, but known, albeit imperfectly, to the soul.

According to Plato, every fleeting experience of beauty we have in this world is a pointer to Beauty Itself. Whenever we gaze upon a rose, or into the eyes of a lover, or up into the starry sky, our souls are being drawn to it.

It sounds fanciful. Ridiculous even. But there's something about it that *feels* right. Because, whether it exists or not, Beauty Itself is precisely what I was grasping for, as a child, when I heard that melody from *Peer Gynt*. And Beauty Itself is what I was grasping at when, as I teenager, I fell in love. And it is something I'm still grasping after today.

Wendy and I arrived, late in the afternoon, at our pub-hotel in Carlops, and spent the evening relaxing hard in preparation for a long walk to Innerleithen.

The following morning, we woke early, washed and dressed, packed our rucksacks, and hurried down to breakfast.

Except that there was no breakfast. Nor any sign of life.

The restaurant and bar were in half-darkness and eerily silent. There were no breakfast places set. No enticing smells wafting in from the kitchen. No pleasant clatter of crockery and pans.

There was no landlord. No waiter. No chef.

Nobody.

It was like waking up on-board the *Mary Celeste*. Or going down to breakfast, post-Rapture, at a motel in Knoxville, Tennessee.

We sat at a table and waited. But nothing happened. So I got up and peeked into the kitchen, which was empty and dark.

On my way back to the table, I spotted some boxes of cereal, some milk, and some cartons of juice on the bar counter. Beside them was a note explaining that the chef was unable to come in that morning. It instructed us to help ourselves to cereal, deduct ten per cent from our bill, leave payment . . . and be on our way.

I had the feeling – perhaps wrongly – that the note had been scribbled in haste by someone anxious to avoid any interaction with possibly disgruntled guests.

Sadly, the cereals were all of the chocolate/honey/sugar-coated varieties that are inedible to persons above eight years old. So I scribbled a note of my own, leaving my email address and telephone number, and offering to negotiate a fair price for our breakfastless stay. I never did hear from them. But my offer still stands.

From Carlops, we continued southeast, taking a rambling route for twenty-four miles to **Innerleithen**, a small town in the Scottish Borders.

During the morning, we walked for ten miles across a sparsely populated area of farmland and woodland. It had few footpaths, and so we had to cobble together a route from any bits of minor road we could find that went in vaguely the right direction.

At midday, we arrived at Eddleston, our first village of the day. From there we'd intended to walk along a dismantled railway, alongside the rivers Eddleston Water and Tweed, to Innerleithen.

Unfortunately, we couldn't *find* the railway path. The bits that were marked as such on the map seemed to have been transformed into houses and gardens in the real world. So, rather than enjoying a congenial riverside walk, we had to slog fourteen miles along the uncongenial A703.

It wasn't a great day, especially since we didn't find a shop where we could buy 'breakfast' until we passed through the town of Peebles, midway through the afternoon.

That night, we stayed on a campsite at the edge of Innerleithen, beside the River Tweed. This was actually rather nice since the town is surrounded by some pretty hills. So the day ended pleasantly.

From there, we walked seventeen miles along a cycle route, following the winding course of the River Tweed, to **Melrose**: a small town that lies adjacent to the larger town of Galashiels.

For Wendy, this was a pleasant riverside walk through woods and fields and across moorland hills. But for me it was a day of blister-agony, especially the last couple of urban miles through Galashiels and Melrose to our campsite.

Although we had walked for only three days since leaving Edinburgh, I had to take a rest day at Melrose. My feet hurt so badly that, apart from hobbling a few hundred yards to a café, I barely moved for the entire time.

In my walking-induced meditative state, I not only listened to music the way I did when I was a teenager, I read that way too.

Throughout JoGLE, while lying in my sleeping-bag at night, I would read a chapter or two of *War and Peace*. And, as the journey progressed, I felt more and more in tune with what Tolstoy had to say.

Whenever I read a novel, it's my practice to highlight any passage that moves or inspires me. And by this stage of my journey I'd highlighted scores of passages from *War and Peace*. Every few pages I came across something that made me mentally exclaim, 'Yes – I see it too!'

This made me recall being nineteen or twenty years old, and lying on my bed, one evening, reading J.D. Salinger's *Franny and Zooey*.

When I reached the final section, where Franny, who is having some kind of breakdown, learns the great secret that pulls her back from the abyss – namely that the 'Fat Lady' is Christ himself – I experienced a kind of ecstasy.

Like all intense aesthetic experiences, it's impossible to describe except by analogy. It was as though something had expanded inside my chest, as though my soul had floated up out of my body, as though a door inside me had been unlocked.

I'd been an avid reader since I was five years old, and had loved and enjoyed hundreds of books. But, until that moment, I'd never imagined that a book, a story, a collection of words, could do that to someone.

The same thing – the expansion of the chest, the floating of the soul, the unlocking of the door – has happened to me, more than once, while listening to Kate Bush.

For example, I recall listening to the *Hounds of Love* album, one time, and somehow the experience became transcendental. The words, the music, the emotion, and the sound of her voice began to resonate – to *throb* – inside me. I was transported.

Both of these experiences were, I believe, examples of what the Ancient Greek rhetorician Longinus labelled 'the sublime'.

In his essay *Of the Sublime*, Longinus observes that certain works of poetry and rhetoric have the power not just to entertain us or to convince us, but to ravish us, to transport us.

'Great writing,' he says, 'does not persuade; it takes the reader out of himself.' It 'commits a pleasing rape upon the very soul of the reader'.

Works of such quality and power, Longinus claims, can proceed only from writers of genius: those with elevated and impassioned spirits, with grand and lofty ideas, and with the ability to communicate all of this through the inspired use of words, rhythms, and figures of speech.

Of course, the experience of the sublime depends not only upon the qualities of the writer, but also upon the qualities of the reader.

I see it this way. When Salinger wrote *Franny and Zooey*, he had a profound insight throbbing inside him. This wasn't something he could express directly, but only through the medium of a story, through the interplay of various characters, through certain rhythms and figures of speech.

My nineteen- or twenty-year-old self was receptive and sympathetic to this idea, was already, in a sense, grasping for it. But it required Salinger's genius, passion, plotting, characterization, and inspired use of language to bring it to birth.

Similarly, on those occasions when Kate Bush's music has transported me, it's because somehow, through her inspired use of words, music, sounds, and images, she has caused something deep within her own soul to resonate with something deep inside mine.

And there, on JoGLE, the same thing was happening with Tolstoy. The combination of his genius and my receptiveness enabled me to appreciate, in a deep way, the sublimity of his work.

For the next stage of our journey, from Melrose to **Jedburgh**, we could have taken an eighteen-mile scenic route along St Cuthbert's Way: a sixty-two-mile walking trail that begins at Melrose and ends at the island of Lindisfarne, off the Northumberland coast, in England.

However, my feet were so tender that we opted for a more direct route instead. This took us thirteen miles, mostly along nondescript minor roads, but also along a section of Dere Street, an old Roman road.

Dere Street originally ran between *Eboracum* (York) and *Inchtuthil* near present-day Falkirk. A lot of it still exists today in the form of A-roads, but the section we walked is now a tree-lined grassy track that passes through Ancrum Moor, where the Scots won a notable victory over the English in 1545.

This four-mile section of the walk was a real treat, but it would be difficult to explain why. It was a dead-straight walk through rough pasture. It passed by a few farms, a couple of streams, a pond or two, and the occasional gnarled old tree. Nothing special when you come to analyse it. But somehow, it just *was* fabulous.

It was while passing through Ancrum Moor that Wendy and I first started to play 'Fives': a conversation game that kept us entertained, on and off, all the way from Melrose to Land's End.

The 'game', if it deserves that title, was simplicity itself. We just picked a category – footpaths, animals, real ales, shower blocks, or whatever – and together compiled a list of the top or bottom five, so far, on JoGLE.

We *loved* that game. And a large part of the reason we loved it is because, by that time, we'd both become such pleasant companions.

In a letter to his niece, Kierkegaard wrote: 'I had been walking for an hour and a half and had done a great deal of thinking, and with the help of motion had really become a very agreeable person to myself.'

In a similar way, during the scores of hours that we had been in motion since leaving John o'Groats, Wendy and I had become very agreeable persons to ourselves – and, consequently, to each other.

It was odd, really. You would think that spending every hour of every day together for such an extended period of time might have made us bored and irritable with one another. And, in normal circumstances, perhaps it might have done. But, out there in the countryside, it didn't. Quite the reverse.

Walking through the countryside, getting plenty of fresh air and exercise, and escaping from the workaday cares and stresses of life, brought out the nicer, more agreeable people inside us.

Wendy sometimes assures me that there's a generous and caring person inside my moody, taciturn exterior. And it was one of JoGLE's most unexpected pleasures, for me – and perhaps for her – to see him emerge.

Although the walk from Melrose hadn't been a long one, it had – thanks to my tender feet – been a slow one. So it was early evening by the time we arrived at Jedburgh.

Jedburgh is an attractive town, situated just ten miles north of the Scottish/English border. It has a ruined abbey, a castle jail, shops, cafés, riverside walks, and whatnot. But Wendy and I passed straight through it to the busy camping site nearby.

From Jedburgh, our plan had been to walk northeast along St Cuthbert's Way to Kirk Yetholm, at the northern end of the Pennine Way.

However, mindful of the days we had lost, due to Wendy's trashed feet, on the first stage of our journey, and mindful of the fact that we wanted to finish JoGLE by mid-October when the autumn weather would begin to bite, we decided instead to head southeast and pick up the Pennine Way at the village of **Byrness**, in England.

This shortcut enabled us to claw back two days of lost time, but at the cost of having to endure a nineteen-mile slog along the A68 to Byrness.

The highlight of the walk was stopping for Mars bars and coffee at a snack-bar called The Borderer, on a concrete layby on the A68, at the Scottish/English border.

The day – and the fourth stage of JoGLE – ended very pleasantly, though, with our arrival at the Forest View Inn, in Byrness.

This former YHA hostel is managed by a retirement-aged couple, Joyce and Colin, who offer free camping in their garden to backpackers who agree to purchase their evening meals at the inn.

Wendy and I knew we had stumbled upon somewhere special the moment we arrived. We were greeted by Colin, who sat us down in the conservatory with tea and biscuits while he scuttled off to clean and dry our boots.

We had expected that camping in the inn's grounds would be a rough-and-ready affair. But to our surprise we found that campers (and Wendy and I were the only two) got a nice, clean bathroom, with hot shower, to themselves.

Throw into the mix a warm lounge with comfy chairs, a three-course meal, draft ale, and the convivial company of slightly tipsy fellow hikers, and you'll understand why we look back on Forest View with enormous affection.

Standing on the bare ground – my head bathed by the blithe air, and uplifted into infinite space – all mean egotism vanishes. I become a transparent eye-ball; I am nothing; I see all.

———————

—RALPH WALDO EMERSON, *NATURE*

CHAPTER FIVE

Getting There

Byrness – Bellingham – Once Brewed –
Greenhead – Alston – Dufton – Langdon
Beck – Baldersdale – Keld – Hawes – Horton
in Ribblesdale – Airton – Skipton – Cowling –
Hebden Bridge – Standedge – Crowden

THE HAPHAZARD ROUTE WENDY AND I HAD TAKEN FROM
Milngavie to Byrness had been largely forgettable. But the next
stage of our journey certainly wasn't.

The Pennine Way, Britain's oldest and most celebrated
National Trail, steers a 267-mile course through some of the
wildest, remotest, and most captivating countryside you could
ever hope to see.

It stretches from Kirk Yetholm, just inside the Scottish
Borders, to Edale in Derbyshire, winding its way through the
Northumberland National Park, the Yorkshire Dales, and the
Peak District National Park. For most of its length, it follows
the line of the Pennines, a range of mountains and hills forming
the 'backbone' of the north of England.

Because of its remoteness, because of the varied and often
difficult nature of its terrain, and because of the extremes of
weather encountered in its high and wild places, it's the most

challenging of all of the National Trails. But it's also – for those very reasons – the most rewarding.

Wendy and I joined the Pennine Way at Byrness rather than at Kirk Yetholm. This meant that we missed the first twenty-nine miles of the trail. But, being End to Enders rather than Pennine-Wayers, we were able to do this with a clear conscience.

End to Enders are honour-bound to walk a continuous line between John o'Groats and Land's End. But apart from that, anything goes.

Our first day's hike along the Pennine Way took us sixteen miles across farmland and moors, and along forest tracks, from **Byrness** to the village of **Bellingham**.

Although the walking was fairly level, it was slow and difficult because there was often no clear path, and because of the mud and the water.

My clearest memories of that day are of wet boots and sodden socks, of slipping and squelching along muddy forest paths, of sinking ankle-deep in moorland bogs, and of frequent backtracking and rerouting to find tolerably firm ground.

It soon became clear that the Pennine Way was going to be much tougher than either the Great Glen Way or the West Highland Way.

We spent the night at a busy campsite, just past Bellingham, and then set off, the next morning, on a fifteen-mile trek along yet more squelchy forest tracks and boggy moorlands to **Once Brewed**, a tiny village consisting of a youth hostel, the confusingly named Twice Brewed Inn, and a smattering of farms.

A few miles short of Once Brewed, the Pennine Way joins the Hadrian's Wall Path for a time. This part of the route requires a lot of scrambling up and down crags. So, by the time we reached the Once Brewed YHA, we were worn out, physically and mentally.

The hostel, which was soon to be demolished and replaced by a state-of-the-art eco-hostel, was in a tired and tatty condition. But a real bed is a real bed, a comfy chair is a comfy chair, and a hot shower is a hot shower. So we weren't complaining.

For the seven miles between Once Brewed and the village of **Greenhead**, the Pennine Way continues to share a route with the Hadrian's Wall Path.

This is a notoriously tough section, with steep ascents and descents over hills and crags. But it's delightful. For much of the way, the path runs alongside exposed sections of the old Roman wall and past the remains of ancient turrets and milecastles. These add interest and drama to the walk.

Furthermore, because the route follows the top of a ridge, it offers glorious views of the surrounding countryside: a green patchwork of hills, fields, and forests, stretching away for an immense distance before meeting the sky.

We set up camp, early in the afternoon, on the grass outside
a campers' barn close to the ruins of twelfth-century Thirlwall
Castle, and then passed a couple of pleasant hours in the
tea-room at nearby Greenhead.

That night, the sky was clear and moonless. So I stayed up, past
midnight, lying on a picnic bench beside our tent, gazing up at
the stars.

Andromeda lay in the east, stretching out an imploring arm
towards Perseus. The Great Bear stood low in the north, watching the Herdsman sink below the northwestern horizon.
Directly overhead, Cygnus, the swan, stretched out his massive
wings and glided silently along the Milky Way. The Andromeda
nebula, 2.5 million light-years distant, stood out clearly: a tiny
luminescent cloud in an ink-black sky.

After a while, I stopped constellation-hopping, switched off
my brain, and simply gazed upwards. It was beautiful. Not just
everyday beautiful, but Plato-beautiful. Beautiful with a capital
'B' – almost.

I often lie out and look at the stars. And, whenever I do, I
experience the same longing I felt as a child, listening to the
opening notes of *Peer Gynt*.

Of all the sights the world affords, no other brings me half
as close to the divine, to the perfect and the unchanging, to
Beauty Itself.

But there's something else too: a curious inner trembling,
an unsettling but oddly comforting sense of being lost in

something vast, a strangely uplifting sense of loneliness and insignificance.

In the past, I have wondered if this experience is peculiar to me. But, of course, it isn't. It is, in fact, an experience common enough to have acquired a label. The same label that Longinus used when discussing great works of poetry and rhetoric: *the sublime*.

In the seventeenth and eighteenth centuries, wealthy young gentlemen would often round off their education by embarking on a Grand Tour of Europe, and steeping themselves in the art and culture of the Renaissance and classical antiquity.

These tours inevitably required them to cross the Alps. And, although, at first, these mountain crossings were considered to be arduous, albeit necessary inconveniences, over time they came to be viewed as highlights of the Tour.

The immensity and grandeur of the peaks, their inaccessibility and remoteness, their formless, chaotic beauty, the sense of danger they evoked, their utter imperviousness to human plans and desires – all of these gave rise to feelings of awe.

In 1688, in a letter describing a walking tour of the Alps, the English critic and dramatist John Dennis wrote that 'the sense of all this produc'd different motions in me, viz. a delightful Horrour, a terrible Joy, and at the same time that I was infinitely pleased, I trembled'.

In the same letter, he took the term *the sublime*, which had previously been used only in discussions of rhetoric and literature, and used it to label this intense aesthetic experience.

A number of British writers, such as Shaftesbury, Joseph

Addison, Edmund Burke, and Hildebrand Jacob, later developed this idea of the sublime as a quality in nature.

In a 1735 essay entitled 'How the mind is raised to the sublime', Hildebrand Jacob listed some of the objects in nature that can evoke a sense of the sublime:

> All the vast, and wonderful scenes, either of delight, or horror, which the universe affords . . . such as unbounded prospects, particularly that of the ocean, in its different situations of agitation, or repose; the rising or setting sun; the solemnity of moon light; all the phaenomena in the heavens, and objects of astronomy. We are moved in the same manner by the view of dreadful precipices; great ruins; subterraneous caverns, and the operations of nature in those dark recesses[.]

The experience of the sublime is one of the most profound that life affords. Lying there, that night, awed by the immensity of space and acutely conscious of my own insignificance, I felt it strongly. And, 'at the same time that I was infinitely pleased, I trembled'.

The twenty-mile section of the Pennine Way from Greenhead to the market town of **Alston** is difficult to navigate, difficult to negotiate, and consists of unremarkable farmland and moorland.

It's difficult to navigate because the waymarks are few and far between, because they don't always point in precisely the right direction, and because they sometimes point in entirely the wrong direction.

Navigational difficulties are made all the more acute if, like Wendy and me, you are travelling from north to south.

There's much talk, in England, of the so-called 'North–South divide' whereby Southerners are said to enjoy all kinds of economic, educational, and cultural advantages over Northerners.

Nowhere is this more apparent than on the Pennine Way. Those walking it from the south have access to any number of guidebooks detailing every step of the way, and benefit from largely adequate signing en route.

Those walking it from the north have access to precisely no guidebooks (it's impossible to gain any useful information by reading a South–North guide backwards), and very often have to make do with signs showing them where they've *been* rather than where they're *going*.

The most remarkable example of North–South bias I saw on the Pennine Way was a notice warning Southerners entering a field to 'Beware of the bull'. This self-same notice served as the only indication to Northerners that they had just *left* a field with a bull in it.

On the day that Wendy and I walked from Greenhead to Alston, our navigational difficulties were further compounded by mist and rain.

The trickiest sections of marsh and moorland on this part of the Pennine Way have no paths. So walkers must rely on a trail of infrequent marker posts to guide their steps. These get swallowed up in the mist and the rain, leaving those without advanced map-and-compass skills blundering around like the biblical madman among the tombs.

The difficulties of negotiation are every bit as great as the difficulties of navigation.

This is first and foremost because large sections of both moorland and farmland here are marshy. So a false step can leave you ankle-deep or knee-deep in water. This necessitates hopping, skipping, and jumping your way from dryish-looking patch to dryish-looking patch, and hoping that those patches really are as dryish as they appear.

There are also places where you have to fight your way through knee-high vegetation that catches at your boots and conceals potentially ankle-breaking rabbit holes.

The cattle also pose problems.

Along the Pennine Way, there are lots of notices warning hikers that cows with calves can become aggressive, and that it's dangerous to walk between a cow and her young. This is no joke. According to the UK's National Office for Statistics, an average of five people per year are trampled to death, and dozens more injured, by cows.

Unfortunately, it's sometimes difficult to avoid getting between a cow and her calves. This is especially true on misty days when you can't see the cows and the cows can't see you.

On this particular day, Wendy and I often found ourselves having to retrace our steps after stumbling across surprised, nervous, or seriously pissed-off-looking cows.

The net result of the rain, the fog, the marshy ground, the knee-high vegetation, the misleading waymarks, and the scary cows was that we made achingly slow progress. At one point, it took us an hour and twenty minutes to cover a single mile.

So, like many End to Enders before us, we abandoned the Pennine Way during the latter part of the day, and walked the last six miles to Alston along the blessedly easy South Tyndale Trail, which follows the route of the old South Tyndale Railway.

Thanks to this sneaky ruse, we arrived at the Alston YHA with plenty of time to relax before bedtime.

Better still, we had set apart the following day as a rest day, and therefore got to spend an additional twenty-four hours in Alston, visiting the shops and cafés on its cobble-stoned main street, and enjoying the fine views of the surrounding fells.

This was a jolly good thing, because the next section of our journey, twenty miles from Alston to **Dufton**, has the reputation of being the Pennine Way's toughest.

We set off at an insanely early hour, anxious to give ourselves plenty of hours of daylight.

The walk began easily and pleasantly enough with a five-mile stretch through farmland and along the banks of the River South Tyne to the tiny village of Garrigill. From there, the Pennine Way winds its way upwards for several miles, across fells and hills, towards the summit of the notorious Cross Fell.

A substantial portion of this three-hour stretch is taken up by the Corpse Path: a steep trail comprised of loose stones, which requires zero navigational skills but is generally detested by hikers because of the heavy toll it takes on the ankles and the knees.

Wendy and I didn't find it too bad. In fact, we quite enjoyed it. Partly because, coming at it from the north, we were walking uphill, which is easier on the joints than walking downhill. Partly because the weather was good. But mostly because, having psyched ourselves up for a long and gruelling day, we were making surprisingly swift and straightforward progress.

Things took a dramatic turn for the worse, however, when we reached Cross Fell and began to make our way across high ground to Great Dun Fell and beyond.

At 2,930 feet, Cross Fell is the highest point on the Pennine Way and the highest point in England outside the Lake District. At 2,782 feet, Great Dun Fell is not much lower.

The region between these two peaks suffers some of the worst weather in Britain, with mist on two hundred days a year, gale-force winds on a hundred days a year, and a mean annual temperature of just four degrees Celsius.

The weather on the ascent had been warm and sunny. But at the summit everything changed. We fought our way from Cross Fell to Great Dun Fell through a gale so strong that it blew us over more than once, through mist so thick that we could barely see one another, and through blinding, stinging rain.

Although it was the middle of summer, we had to raid our rucksacks for fleece jumpers, waterproofs, hats, and gloves to protect ourselves from the cold.

The route here is ill-defined and tricky to navigate. In some of the boggiest places, there are paths made from stone slabs, but apart from that it's a matter of walking between man-made piles of stones known as cairns.

In such poor weather, these cairns are invisible, and not even the best map-and-compass skills can save you from constant blundering and backtracking.

In the end, I had to place my entire faith in my smartphone's GPS. 'The GPS says we're west of the trail,' I would say to Wendy, shouting to make myself heard above the gale. 'So we have to go *this* way . . .'

In this manner, we battled our way to Great Dun Fell and beyond, stopping inside a low-walled stone shelter, part way across, for a few minutes' blessed relief from the wind.

After Great Dun Fell, there's a brief descent, followed by a final climb to the summit of Knock Old Man. After this, the trail leads steadily downwards for five miles to Alston.

This descent, though tough on the knees, was a pleasure and a delight. With each step, the wind dropped, the mist thinned, and the temperature rose.

Being an inexperienced walker, it came as a glorious surprise to me to discover that beneath the summits, below the cloud line, lay a world still bathed in warmth and sunshine: a wholesome, joyful, welcoming world.

We arrived at the YHA in Dufton – a quintessentially English village centred upon a splendid old-fashioned village green – in great good humour, having conquered the longest and toughest section of the Pennine Way.

By this stage, I had become aware that the beauty of the Pennine Way is of a very different sort than the beauty of the Great Glen Way and the West Highland Way.

The beauty of those other trails – at least, insofar as Wendy and I experienced them – is predominantly of a gentle, harmonious kind. It's the beauty of green meadows and rolling hills, of purple-flowering heather and yellow-flowering broom, of tranquil lakes and gurgling streams, and of forest paths dappled in sunlight.

But the beauty of the Pennine Way is often harsh and discordant, and, at times, not unmixed with a trace of ugliness. It's the beauty of marshes and bogs, of jagged rocks and formless crags, of meagre trees on windswept moors, of fearful cascades, and of mist-shrouded peaks.

The landscapes of the Great Glen Way and the West Highland Way are beautiful in a way that evokes feelings of tranquillity and pleasure, whereas the landscapes of the Pennine Way have more of the sublime about them. They too give pleasure, but of a more acute kind, which stimulates as often as it soothes the mind.

Earlier in my journey, I had asked myself what it is that makes the countryside so soothing to the spirit and so refreshing to the soul. But the question had proved too deep and difficult for me to make much progress with it. Fortunately, however, finer intellects than mine have tackled the same question with greater success. Most notably, Schopenhauer.

Like many nineteenth-century intellectuals, Schopenhauer weighed in on the then fashionable debate about the beautiful and the sublime, and the way we experience them. His account runs as follows.

When we encounter a beautiful object, such as a flower or a mountain lake, we may, if we are in a suitable frame of mind, lose ourselves in contemplation of it. At such times, our ego, our desire, our will, is temporarily quieted. We appreciate the object not for what it is in relation to ourselves, but simply for what it is in itself. We take a disinterested pleasure in it.

For as long as this aesthetic experience lasts, we are freed from our ordinary, self-conscious way of apprehending the world. We enjoy, for a time, the profound tranquillity of will-less contemplation.

But when we encounter the sublime – perhaps when gazing up into a starry sky or looking out over the edge of a precipice – the experience is more complex.

Sublime objects have something about them that is hostile to the human will, something that overpowers, or threatens, or overwhelms, something of pain or fear. They have a kind of beauty – often breath-taking in its intensity – but it is a terrible beauty.

Such things reveal to us the smallness and insignificance of ourselves, our wills, and our desires. In doing so, they enable us, for a time, to abandon ourselves, and to give ourselves over to the world.

When we contemplate the sublime, we don't so much forget ourselves as free ourselves. We don't lose consciousness of the will and its desires, but instead are liberated from them. And this gives rise to a kind of rapture, to, in Schopenhauer's words, a 'state of elevation'.

If all of this sounds a bit fanciful and overblown, I can state quite categorically, from my own experience, that it isn't. It describes *exactly* the way I feel when I gaze up at the stars. On the one hand, I am conscious of myself and my cares and my desires, but, on the other hand, I am blissfully conscious that they don't amount to a hill of beans.

From Dufton, the Pennine Way heads in an easterly direction for thirteen miles to **Langdon Beck**.

For JoGLErs, like Wendy and me, this section of the Way is a complete waste of time and effort in a purely goal-orientated sense, since Langdon Beck is actually further away from Land's End than Dufton is. But, despite this, we enjoyed it immensely.

The walk, as a whole, was a pleasant one across high moors and pastures, between fells, and along the banks of Maize Beck and the River Tees. And in addition to all of the general pleasantness there were a number of special delights.

A few miles from Dufton, the path ascends steeply and then traverses for a mile or two along the northwestern rim of High Cup, a gigantic U-shaped glacial valley. This geological wonder, which looks like a colossal grass-covered meteor scar, is one of the scenic highlights of the entire Pennine Way.

The path continues to High Cup Nick, the apex of the valley, where Wendy and I stopped for a mid-morning break to enjoy the stunning view of High Cup stretching away below us.

After that, we walked a further five miles across the fells, arriving early in the afternoon at Cauldron Snout, Britain's longest waterfall. We sat there for a long time, eating lunch and watching the River Tees blast its way with explosive force through a series of rocky cataracts. Finally, we hiked the last few miles to our destination, the YHA at the tiny hamlet of Langdon Beck. This took quite some time, since this part of the route includes a lengthy, physically demanding scramble along a boulder-lined section of the River Tees.

All in all, the day's walk had been one of JoGLE's most scenic, exhilarating, and satisfying so far. And, to cap it all, we arrived at the hostel to find a freshly baked Victoria sponge cake sitting on the kitchen counter-top, alongside a notice reading, 'HELP YOURSELF'.

We later found out that it had been baked by the mother of one of the hostel staff, for no other reason than to spread a little happiness.

God bless her.

The journey from Langdon Beck to **Baldersdale** was just fifteen miles long, but it felt like fifty.

It began innocuously enough with a gentle walk along the River Tees past two sets of waterfalls: the modest but pretty Low Force, where the river drops eighteen feet along a series of shallow steps, and the anything-but-modest High Force, where the river plunges noisily and spectacularly over a seventy-one-feet precipice.

We stopped for lunch at the small market town of Middleton-in-Teesdale, somehow resisting the lure of the cafés and teashops, and making do with crisps and pre-packaged sandwiches from the Co-op instead. And from there, we set off, first across Harter Fell and then across Mickleton Moor, to Baldersdale.

In theory, this should have been a straightforward jaunt across undulating moorland and rough pasture. But, in practice, it turned out to be a long and bitter battle against the wind.

A five-minute walk into a strong wind is bracing. A thirty-minute walk into a strong wind is tiring. But a three-hour walk into a strong wind is *bloody exhausting*.

Our original plan had been to walk four or five miles past the valley of Baldersdale to the village of Bowes. But the wind had sapped our energy and impeded our progress so much that we were glad to hole up for the evening at Baldersdale, in a bunk-house at the remote Clove Lodge Cottage.

Wendy and I had the six-bedded bunkhouse at Clove Lodge, with its kitchen, lounge, dining area, toilet, and shower, to ourselves. It was lovely.

After cooking and eating dinner, we settled ourselves into comfy chairs in front of the wood-burning stove, gazed into the fire flames, and cared not a fig for the wind howling across the dark moors outside.

It was around this time that a curious thing happened to me. I began, against all of my expectations, to take pleasure in the problems and challenges of the trail.

Don't misunderstand me. I didn't derive immediate enjoyment from picking my way across marshes, blundering through mists and gales, or slithering, rain-soaked, across slippery rocks. But I did take pleasure in pitting myself against these obstacles, day after day, and overcoming them.

In the past, the walks I always enjoyed best were what I call 'teashop' walks: pleasant ambles through summer glades with pubs and cafés to break the monotony. So I was taken by surprise to discover that the Pennine Way, with its myriad pitfalls and privations, had become the most enjoyable part of JoGLE so far.

From somewhere in the depths of my mind, a half-remembered quote from the Austrian psychiatrist and Holocaust survivor Viktor Frankl resurfaced. I checked it out on Google and found that it comes from his book *Man's Search for Meaning*, and that it goes like this: 'What man actually needs is not a tensionless state but rather the striving and struggling for some goal worthy of him.'

Frankl was the founder of *logotherapy*: a form of psychotherapy based on his belief that the striving for meaning is the most powerful and motivating force in human life, and that a sense of purpose is essential to mental wellbeing.

He acquired these beliefs partly as a result of his observations and experiences as a prisoner in the Nazi concentration camps in WWII, and partly as a result of his psychiatric practice later in life.

In the concentration camps, he observed that those prisoners who held onto a sense of meaning amidst their suffering were more likely to survive than those who did not. And in his psychiatric practice, he noticed that what was missing, above all else, in the lives of many depressed and suicidal men and women was a sense of purpose: a goal or cause to which they could dedicate themselves wholeheartedly.

Frankl held that without a deeply felt sense of purpose even the most comfortable lives can feel sad and empty, and with such a sense of purpose even the most outwardly wretched lives can feel worthwhile.

'Those who have a "why" to live,' he said, quoting Nietzsche, 'can bear almost any "how".'

The precise nature of this 'why' varies from individual to individual. Life's meaning can be found in raising a family, creating a work of art, advancing the cause of science, excelling at sport, serving the community, achieving financial success, or communing with nature. The essential thing, as far as mental wellbeing is concerned, is that the individual is committed to some freely chosen goal that is replete with meaning for him- or herself.

Of course, the pursuit of any worthwhile goal brings with it some tension. Nothing meaningful is ever achieved without a struggle. But, according to Frankl, such tension is an indispensable prerequisite of psychological wellbeing.

He writes: 'Thus it can be seen that mental health is based on a certain degree of tension, the tension between what one has already achieved and what one still ought to accomplish.'

Frankl's ideas summed up precisely how I was beginning to feel about JoGLE.

Had JoGLE been nothing but a succession of teashop walks, it would have been easy, it would have been comfortable, and it would have been horribly dull. But, instead, it had turned out to be difficult and challenging. And that's what made it interesting and worthwhile.

For me, JoGLE contained precisely the right amount of tension between past achievement and future accomplishment. On any given day, I could look back with satisfaction on the miles I had already covered and the difficulties I had already overcome. And, at the same time, I could look forward with eager anticipation to the miles I had yet to cover and the difficulties I had yet to overcome.

For this brief period of my life, I had committed myself wholeheartedly to a single, freely chosen goal: that of walking from John o'Groats to Land's End. And each day gave me the opportunity to progress towards that goal.

In a sense, JoGLE had become, for me, a taste of what life *could* be and what life *ought* to be. It had provided me with an escape – or, at least, a respite – from a sense of meaninglessness, which for years had cast a shadow over my life.

It began like this.

In my early to mid-thirties, I entered a new and unpleasant phase of life, which I wrongly assumed would be a passing one.

Each night, as I lay in bed waiting for sleep, with the day's business and the day's pleasures behind me, I would fall prey to a nagging sense of unease. I couldn't identify any cause. I had no specific worries. I just felt vaguely depressed and dissatisfied. Even a little afraid.

The next morning, and all through the following afternoon and evening, I would feel perfectly normal again. But come night-time, the unease, the depression, and the anxiety would return.

At one point in *Man's Search for Meaning*, Viktor Frankl refers to a psychological condition he calls 'Sunday neurosis': a form of depression that affects people when the busyness of the week subsides and their inner emptiness surfaces.

Looking back, I would say that I was suffering from something very much like that. But at the time I had very little insight into the problem. I knew that when I had nothing to occupy my thoughts I felt sad. But I didn't understand why.

All of this would have been of little account, and hardly worth mentioning, except for the fact that, contrary to expectations, the feeling never entirely left me.

There were times, for example when I took a break from teaching to study philosophy, or when I first achieved some small successes as a writer, when I thought it had gone for good. But once the novelty of a new project or a new interest had worn off, the void would reopen – and each time a little wider than before.

By the time, I set off on JoGLE, at the age of forty-nine, the sense of meaninglessness and unease had become chronic. The void had become a more or less permanent feature of my inner life, and I had begun to doubt whether anything could fill it.

But strangely and wonderfully, the simple act of walking through the countryside every day, and slowly making progress towards Land's End, brought back long-unaccustomed feelings of cheerfulness and contentment.

We set off from Clove Lodge, the next morning, on a fourteen-mile hike from Baldersdale to the village of **Keld**. This began with a three-mile stretch across Cotherstone Moor: an extensive area of peat bog covered with low woody shrubs and tough grasses.

At the southern edge of Cotherstone Moor, the Pennine Way crosses the A69, and shortly afterwards crosses the River Greta by means of God's Bridge, Britain's finest natural limestone bridge.

It was a sunny, mildly breezy day, and Wendy I were tempted by the weather, and by the picturesque beauty of the rocky riverbank and the surrounding meadows, to stop and rest. This gave us ample time to admire the structure of the bridge, which, with its huge, neatly laid, horizontal slabs, looks for all the world as though it really has been constructed by divine hands.

From God's Bridge, the path heads across Wytham Moor, Bowes Moor, and Sleightholme Moor to the remote Tan Hill Inn, the highest inn in the British Isles.

The moors here are boggy, criss-crossed by streams and covered in heather. Progress across them is often achingly slow because the track frequently vanishes into the heather, and because the ground is so boggy that there's a constant risk of sinking waist-deep – or worse – into the mire.

Wendy and I had walked this section of the Pennine Way once before during a particularly wet summer, and had had a very bad – not to say scary – time of it. Consequently, I had been dreading this crossing for days. However, thanks to the unusually dry summer, this time around we crossed it quickly and easily.

I don't suppose there has ever been, in the fifty-year history of the Pennine Way, a hiker who has walked straight on past the Tan Hill Inn. Nobody, surely, could resist the lure of beer, food, and shelter in such a wild, windswept, and lonely location.

Wendy and I stepped inside for a pint of beer and a packet of crisps, and then stayed on for a second pint of beer and an additional packet of crisps. Then, feeling slightly tipsy, and disinclined to exert ourselves any more than was absolutely necessary, we exercised our prerogative as End to Enders and abandoned the Pennine Way to follow a small road to our campsite at Keld, four miles away.

Keld is a pretty little village, nestled among some modest hills in the Yorkshire Dales, and has the distinction of being the crossing point of the Pennine Way and the Coast to Coast Walk.

Sadly, we timed our arrival there to coincide with a plague of midges of biblical proportions. So we were not sorry, the following morning, to pack up our tent and move on.

The eleven-mile hike from Keld to the small market town of **Hawes** began with a tiring section along the steep rock-strewn valley of the River Keld.

Here, a combination of fatigue and inattention caused me to take a slip on some wet rocks. In the resulting fall, the screen of our tablet computer, our main navigational tool, was cracked. Fortunately, it still worked, and, thanks to Wendy's judicious application of duct tape, it lasted us all the way to Land's End.

After stopping for coffee at the village of Thwaite, we set off across hilly moorland, then up and over Great Shunner Fell, one of the highest points on the Pennine Way, then through the tiny hamlet of Hardraw, and finally through meadows and pastures to our campsite, just outside Hawes.

Hawes is the highest market town in England. It's situated at the western end of the Wensleydale valley, and surrounded on all sides by moorland fells. It's a pretty little place with a handsome main street of stone-built houses, and with some nice little shops and cafés and inns.

We arrived during a spell of beautiful warm weather, and made the most of it by taking a rest day there, which we spent doing laundry, mooching around the shops, enjoying cream teas, and lazing around on the grass beside our tent. It was good.

Walking JoGLE had given me a new sense of purpose in life, and this had led to my feeling uncharacteristically cheerful and contented. Sceptically minded readers might object that walking from Land's End to John o'Groats isn't, in the great scheme of things, much of a purpose. Not like seeking a cure for cancer, or writing a symphony, or stamping out racism, or snatching sinners from the jaws of Hell, or something of that sort.

But that's not really the point. As far as happiness and flourishing are concerned, the purpose to which an individual commits need not be of a kind that counts for much *in the great scheme of things*. It need only be freely chosen and replete with personal meaning. It can be a great or a small enterprise; a public or a private one; a long-term or a short-term one.

In *Man's Search for Meaning*, Viktor Frankl writes:

The meaning of life differs from man to man, from day to day and from hour to hour. What matters, therefore, is not the meaning of life in general but rather the specific meaning of a person's life at a given moment.

And for me, at that time, the simple act of walking a thousand-plus miles from John o'Groats to Land's End had become meaningful. Not in a grand and cosmic sense. Not 'in the great scheme of things'. But meaningful to *me*.

The next section of the Pennine Way, from Hawes to **Horton in Ribblesdale**, was a fifteen-mile journey across rough pastureland and lonely moors. It was fairly easy walking, and included some long, easy-to-navigate stretches along old drove roads and old Roman roads.

It was cold when we arrived, and looked like it was about to rain. So we decided that, rather than cooking and eating dinner alfresco, we would treat ourselves to a pub meal and a pint or two of beer.

There are two pubs in Horton in Ribblesdale: The Crown and the Golden Lion. We strolled first to The Crown where we were greeted with a dazzling array of notices, printed on A4 paper, informing guests how best to conduct themselves with a view to the mutual convenience and satisfaction of all parties:

NO MUDDY BOOTS

NO DOGS

DO NOT SIT AROUND THE FIRE

DO NOT DRY YOUR COAT NEAR THE FIRE
NO BACKPACKS.

I can't be sure, but I think there may have also been a notice saying something along the lines of: 'WHY DON'T YOU WALKERS TAKE YOUR FILTHY BOOTS, SMELLY DOGS AND DIRTY GREAT BACKPACKS AND FECK OFF OUT OF HERE?'

In any case, we did feck off out of there, and had a gigantic and delicious Yorkshire pudding with roast beef, peas, and gravy at the slightly down-at-heel but perfectly welcoming Golden Lion.

The following morning, Wendy and I woke early to the sound of rain. I checked the weather forecast and saw that it was set to continue for most of the day. There was no point waiting for a dry spell, so we took down our tent in the rain, packed it into our rucksacks in the rain, and then set off walking in the rain.

From Horton in Ribblesdale, the Pennine Way takes a circuitous route to the village of Malham, and includes a steep climb over Pen-y-Ghent, an imposing fell that rises abruptly out of the surrounding countryside.

Pen-y-Ghent is considered quite a challenging peak. Wendy and I had climbed it once before, and remembered that it was rocky and exposed in places, and required a fair bit of scrambling. We didn't fancy clambering over those treacherous rocks in the rain, especially not with heavy backpacks. So we elected to abandon the Pennine Way for the day, and instead take a thirteen-mile hike along small roads to the village of **Airton**.

I remember little about the day's walk, except that we passed through some very tough-looking country and that it was very, very wet.

There's no campsite at Airton, and so we splashed out and stayed at a farmhouse B&B. We were greeted at the door by an attractive young woman and two very lively young children. When the woman handed us the keys to our room, the oldest child, aged about four, informed us that it was a very *good* room because it had a very *bouncy* bed. Both children then accompanied us upstairs and gave us a practical demonstration of the elastic and gymnastic possibilities of our mattress.

The Pennine Way passes through Airton. So, the next morning, we re-joined it, intending to follow it all the way to the village of Cowling.

Unfortunately, after just four miles, as we passed through the village of Gargrave, I felt a stabbing pain in the small of my back. I tore off my rucksack and found that a thin metal rod, which formed part of the frame, had punctured the fabric and transformed itself into a lethal weapon.

It was impossible to continue like that. So we were forced to take a detour off the Pennine Way, and follow the Leeds and Liverpool Canal to the town of **Skipton** – which, as luck would have it, was situated just four miles away.

We arrived at Skipton, purchased a new rucksack, and then walked southeast for a few miles to re-join the Pennine Way. After that, we headed south across hilly pastures to **Cowling**, where we camped beside a farmhouse B&B, on a sloping field covered in sheep-poo.

The following morning, we set off early on a sixteen-mile hike through Brontë country to the market town of **Hebden Bridge**.

It was a cold, wet walk through some of the most inhospitable moorland in England. Everything that grows there is adapted to survive rather than to thrive. The heather, the grasses, and the few scanty trees are coarse, tough, and self-contained. They give the impression of clinging on doggedly to life rather than embracing it.

The most famous landmark on this section of the Pennine Way, located between the bleak wilderness of Stanbury Moor and the equally bleak wilderness of Wadsworth Moor, is Top Withens, a ruined farmhouse that is said to have been the inspiration for the Earnshaw family home, Wuthering Heights, in Emily Brontë's classic novel.

That *Wuthering Heights* is one of the great works of English literature, I wouldn't dispute for a moment. But personally I don't care for it. It's too bleak, too savage, and too cruel. It disturbs me.

There's a popular misconception – primarily among people who haven't read it, but also, surprisingly, among some people who have – that it's a love story. But it isn't. It's a hate story.

There's passion in it. And there's desire, of a sort. But as far as the principal characters, Catherine and Heathcliff, are concerned – and most of the other characters, come to that – there's little I recognize as love.

Charlotte Brontë, Emily's sister, had it about right, I think, when she described Heathcliff's love for Catherine as 'perverted passion and passionate perversity'.

I've read *Wuthering Heights* three times, and each time I've wondered what prompted Emily to write it. Why introduce so much gratuitous misery into the world?

But walking across those wild and inhospitable moors, that day, I began to understand.

The Brontë family lived in the parsonage in the village of Howarth, which lies within easy reach of Top Withens and the surrounding moors. So Emily would have been intimately acquainted with that harsh and unforgiving landscape. Small wonder, then, that she was inspired to produce such a harsh and unforgiving novel.

In an 1848 edition of the British newspaper *The Examiner*, a reviewer wrote: 'Whoever has traversed the bleak heights of Hartside or Cross Fell . . . and has been welcomed there by the winds and rain on a "gusty day", will know how to estimate the comforts of Wuthering Heights in wintry weather' – which says it all, I think.

From Top Withens, the Pennine Way continues for another six or seven miles across Wadsworth Moor and Heptonstall Moor before passing Hebden Bridge.

Since Wendy and I were spending the night at a hostel in Hebden Bridge, we had to take a mile-and-a-half detour off the

Pennine Way, into town. This turned out to be an exhausting slog, which involved a long steep descent, followed by a series of outrageously steep ups and downs. The initial descent was heart-breaking, since we knew that we would have to make up the height we had lost the following morning, when we returned to the Pennine Way.

Hebden Bridge is a spectacular town: a hotchpotch of imposing stone buildings, cobbled streets, rivers, streams, canals, roads, and railway lines, all crammed into the steep sides of the Upper Calder Valley.

It developed as a mill town in the nineteenth and twentieth centuries, courtesy of its steep hills and fast-flowing streams. Today, thanks to its location halfway between Leeds and Manchester, it's a commuter town, and thanks to its gorgeous stone buildings, cobbled streets, boutiques, and pretty waterways, it also has a thriving tourist industry.

For me, the most charming feature of Hebden Bridge was the improbable steepness of its streets. Charming to look at, that is. But when it came to walking out of town, the next morning, to re-join the Pennine Way, those steep inclines were an absolute bitch.

The seventeen-mile stretch of the Pennine Way from Hebden Bridge to **Standedge** (pronounced *Stannidge*) is perhaps the most tedious section of the Pennine Way. It runs across drab moorland, punctuated only by dull streams, unattractive drains, and un-scenic reservoirs.

End to End blogger Mark Moxon opens his discussion of this section of the Pennine Way with the words: 'Ye gods, what a boring walk!' and goes on to say that the bit where it crosses the M62 motorway is probably the highlight of the whole thing.

I think it's fair to say that these sentiments are echoed by the majority of Pennine Way walkers. However, Wendy and I were fortunate enough to cross it on a misty day, which lent it a pleasing air of mystery and romance.

We arrived, late in the afternoon, at a tiny campsite in the grounds of the Carriage House pub, near Standedge. The weather was cold and damp, and our camping pitch was strewn with soggy litter from the previous occupants. So we decamped into the pub until bedtime.

From Standedge, the Pennine Way heads east across Wessenden Moor, passing alongside a number of small reservoirs, and then bends southward, climbing up through Wessenden Head Moor to the boggy, peaty summit of Black Hill.

Wainwright, the celebrated fell walker and guidebook author, describes Black Hill as his least favourite place on the Pennine Way. 'The broad top really is black,' he says. 'It is not the only fell with a summit of peat but no other shows such a desolate and hopeless quagmire to the sky. This is peat naked and unashamed. Nature fashioned it, but for once has no suggestion for clothing it.'

It's all a matter of taste though. Personally, I like bleak places. I find them exhilarating. And I'm not alone in that respect. Wendy feels the same way. And Thoreau, the nineteenth-century American author, philosopher, and naturalist, went so far as to express a marked preference for the bleak over the picturesque. In his essay *Walking*, he wrote: 'My spirits infallibly rise in proportion to the outward dreariness. Give me the ocean, the desert, or the wilderness!'

From Black Hill, the Pennine Way continues south, and before long reaches Laddow Rocks, an exposed crag that's popular with climbers. Then the path traverses the side of a steep ravine, with a vertigo-inducing drop to Crowden Great Brook below, before descending into **Crowden**.

This was an easy-paced and enjoyable twelve-mile walk until about an hour from the end when the rain began to beat down. The downpour came as no surprise. In this part of the world they have a saying: 'If you can't see the fells, it's raining. If you can see the fells, it's going to rain.' But, although the rain wasn't unexpected, it still dampened our spirits.

The appearance of the campsite at Crowden did little to revive them. Rivulets of water ran down the leaves of the trees and bushes, glistening beads of water clung to the grass, the sides of the tents sagged beneath the weight of water, and still the rain came down.

We set up our wet tent on the wet field, and then squatted outside in our wet raincoats and wet over-trousers, heating up a tin of spaghetti hoops and raindrops.

From Crowden, our original plan had been to continue to the southern end of the Pennine Way, at Edale. But with more rain forecast, and with the hostel and the B&Bs at Edale full, and with no other option at Edale but to camp, we decided that it would be best to abandon the Pennine Way and head instead for the small Derbyshire town of Chapel-en-Le-Frith.

The following morning, as we squatted outside in the rain, scraping fat black slugs from the wet interior of our outer-tent prior to packing it into our wet backpacks, we felt sure that we had made the right decision.

Being End to Enders, we had no guilty qualms about quitting the Pennine Way early. For us, it had only ever been a means to an end, and never an end in itself. But still we felt a tinge of regret as we bade farewell to the moors and the mountains. Because, as means to an end go, it had been pretty bloody magnificent.

I travelled among unknown men,
In lands beyond the sea;
Nor, England! did I know til then
What love I bore to thee.

———————

—WILLIAM WORDSWORTH, 'I TRAVELLED
AMONG UNKNOWN MEN'

CHAPTER SIX

Heart of England

Crowden – Chapel-en-Le-Frith –
Hartington – Dimmingsdale – Little
Haywood – Lichfield – Coleshill – Henley-in-Arden –
Bidford-on-Avon – Dumbleton – Cheltenham –
Painswick – Cam – Old Sodbury – Bath

THE SIXTH STAGE OF OUR END TO END JOURNEY TOOK US south along two long-distance walking trails: the Heart of England Way and the Cotswold Way.

The Heart of England Way runs for about a hundred miles through the Midlands, from Milford Common in Staffordshire to Bourton-on-the-Water in the Cotswolds. It skirts around the eastern rim of Birmingham, England's second-largest city, and passes close to the city of Coventry. But, despite this, it's not at all urban. In fact, for the most part, it feels deeply rural.

Of all of the National Trails, it is – with its woods, pastures, country lanes, canals, orchards, cultivated fields, steepled churches, and sleepy villages – perhaps the most quintessentially English.

The Cotswold Way is England's newest National Trail. It runs 102 miles from Chipping Campden in Gloucestershire to Bath in Somerset. For most of its length, it follows the Cotswold

Edge escarpment, zigzagging its way between the peaks and troughs of the Cotswold Hills.

It is absurdly pretty, running through a sculpted landscape so picturesque that it might have been designed by The Walt Disney Company. Among a host of other delights, it boasts exhilarating high-level views, lush meadows sprinkled with cattle and sheep, shady woodlands, and charming villages with houses of honey-coloured Cotswold stone.

But before Wendy and I could sample any of these delights, we had to spend four days walking an improvised route to the northern end of the Heart of England Way, at Milford Common.

The first instalment, from **Crowden** to **Chapel-en-Le-Frith** began pleasantly enough with a three-mile stretch along the Pennine Way and the Trans Pennine Trail. But after that it was road-walking all the way.

The highlight of the day came mid-morning when we stopped for coffee and cake in the centre of Glossop. Then it was down to business with a long damp trudge along the A624.

There's no campsite near Chapel-en-Le-Frith. So the walk ended with a decadent stay at the Forest Lodge B&B, with a king-size bed, a corner bath, and a hospitality tray stocked with biscuits *and* chocolates.

Our onward journey to the village of **Hartington** was another dull, damp slog. We had intended to walk the first half-dozen miles along minor roads to the spa town of Buxton, and then head off into the moors, along the Midshires Way and the Pennine Bridleway, to Hartington. But the weather was so foul that from Buxton we decided to forget the moors and continue along minor roads, through hilly farmland, to our destination.

For the last few miles, we were walking into driving rain, which proved more than a match for my battered old waterproofs. By the time we arrived at the Hartington YHA, I was wet through and shivering, and had to stand in a hot shower for a full ten minutes before my teeth stopped chattering.

I have remarked more than once, in these pages, upon the fact that on JoGLE, as in life, good times never last, and neither do bad times. 'Weeping may endure for a night,' as the good book says, 'but joy cometh in the morning.'

And at Hartington, joy *did* come in the morning.

Hartington is a pretty little village, situated in the Derbyshire Peak District, close to the Staffordshire border. It has everything an English village should have: a history dating back to the Middle Ages, stone houses and cottages, a sandstone church with a fine tower, a village square complete with duck pond, and a seventeenth-century manor house, Hartington Hall, which is now the YHA.

It's the perfect place for weary, weather-beaten travellers to enjoy a rest day. And that's precisely what Wendy and I did.

And, to cap it all, we had the thrill of posting home fifteen pounds of camping equipment.

The recent run of cold wet weather, which was only likely to worsen as autumn advanced, convinced us that, as far as we were concerned, the camping season was over. Consequently, we were able to lighten our backpacks to the tune of one tent, two sleeping-bags, two sleeping-bag liners, two sleeping-mats, two travel pillows, and sundry items of cooking equipment.

Unburdening ourselves of these items lightened our spirits no less than our backpacks. From that point onwards, there would be no more setting up and taking down camp, no more scraping slugs from the inside of a wet outer-tent, no more early-hours trudges to toilet blocks, and no more crouching over a one-ring burner to cook one-pan meals. Instead, it would be hostels and bed and breakfasts all the way – and budget be damned!

From Hartington, we walked sixteen forgettable miles, along minor roads, and along the banks of the River Manifold and the River Hamps, to **Dimmingsdale**, a forest area in the valley of the River Churnet.

That night, we had the Dimmingsdale YHA, a somewhat Spartan but splendidly isolated woodland retreat, all to ourselves. After dinner, as the evening hours rolled pleasantly and uneventfully by, I remember thinking how glad I was that I had agreed to walk from End to End.

I hadn't set off upon JoGLE in the expectation that it would give me pleasure and make me happy. I had expected it to give *Wendy* pleasure and make *her* happy – and that was a big incentive. But for me, on a purely personal level, it had been about neither pleasure nor happiness. It had been about challenge.

JoGLE, in some vague sense, had seemed to be a challenging and worthwhile thing to do. So I decided to do it. And, having begun it, it never once occurred to me – not for a single moment – to stop.

No matter how footsore I got, or how weary, or how wet, or how bored, I plodded on. Not because I believed that enduring footsoreness, weariness, wetness, and boredom would make me a happier person in the long run, but simply because I knew that enduring those things would get me to Land's End.

But, against all of my expectations, I discovered that plodding on, day after day, concerning myself only with getting to Land's End, and concerning myself not at all with trying to becoming a happier person, I had become a happier person.

The nineteenth-century English philosopher and social reformer John Stuart Mill wrote:

Those only are happy who have their minds fixed on some object other than their own happiness: on the happiness of others, on the improvement of mankind, even on some art or pursuit . . . Aiming thus at something else, they find happiness by the way.

This profound truth – that you can find happiness only when you're not looking for it – was expressed with admirable brevity by the English scientist and novelist C.P. Snow: 'The pursuit of happiness is a ridiculous phrase, if you pursue happiness, you'll never find it.'

This is precisely what I had found, and was learning more and more each day, on JoGLE. The quest to reach Land's End was taking up so much of my time and energy and focus, and was absorbing me so completely, that I had forgotten to ask myself whether I was happy or not. And, as a result, I felt happier than I had done in years.

The next day's walk was another purely functional one, designed to get us from Dimmingsdale to the village of **Little Haywood**, which lies close to the northern end of the Heart of England Way.

Our twenty-mile route took us almost entirely along country roads with the occasional farm track thrown in for good measure, and was memorable only for a couple of canine-related adventures.

The first of these occurred when we had to pass through a farmyard.

I always get nervous when I have to pass through farmyards. On account of the dogs.

There are a small but significant number of farmers (the few bad apples that spoil the bunch, no doubt) who like to use their dogs to deter walkers from passing through their farmyards, or, failing that, to make passing through as unpleasant as possible.

And note that I'm not talking about *trespassers* here. I'm talking about legitimate walkers using public rights of way, including National Trails.

Some of these farmers keep vicious, snarling brutes chained up or caged up, out of sight, in their farmyards. This means that hikers passing that way must either retreat and re-route, or must screw their courage to the sticking place and press on, trusting that the farmer isn't such an out-and-out psychopath that he'd allow them to be torn limb from limb by free-range Rottweilers.

Other farmers allow their dogs to roam freely around the farmyard and molest hikers to their doggy hearts' content. These dogs are never such life-threateningly vicious brutes as the chained-up ones, but are nevertheless perfectly capable of causing injury, should their inclinations ever turn that way.

On this particular day, our route took us through one such farmyard.

My heart sank as we drew near and heard the sound of barking. Moments later, not one but three dogs came tearing towards us and then began leaping up against the farmyard gate and barking at us. They were young dogs – border collies — but quite old enough to bite.

Wendy and I approached them slowly, hoping, but not really expecting, that the farmer would appear to call them off.

He didn't.

I turned to Wendy and grimaced. 'What choice do we have? We have to go through . . .'

I eased open the gate, squeezed through, and entered the

farmyard in what I hoped was a suitably calm and assertive manner. All three dogs immediately set upon me: jumping up, balancing their front paws on my chest, and nuzzling and licking me in an ecstasy of delight.

'Quick! Take a photo!' I said, handing my smartphone to Wendy.

As she fumbled with the controls, I abandoned myself to their canine caresses. It was a beautiful moment.

Then, from a wooden kennel close to the farmhouse, Mother emerged. She lowered her head and shoulders in a ready-to-pounce attitude and gave a low growl that said, in no uncertain terms, 'Leave my kids *the fuck* alone!'

I left her kids *the fuck* alone, and walked swiftly, non-aggressively, and pseudo-calmly through the farmyard and out the other side.

The young dogs, which moments before had been doting and fawning upon me quite shamelessly, now adopted their mother's attitude and posture, and escorted me from the premises with growls, snarls, and bared teeth.

The day's second canine-related adventure occurred an hour or two later. This time while we were walking along a narrow road, near to a small village.

On this occasion, the dog concerned was walking towards us, unleashed, beside a young woman in green wellies and a waxed jacket. As they drew near, the dog, which was a fair-sized beast, came bounding and barking towards us.

Wendy and I had no idea what its intentions were. So we stood quite still, and looked to the young woman for aid.

'Don't worry,' she said, 'he won't bite!'

I wasn't so sure. So, recalling some advice from TV's *The Dog Whisperer*, I held out my hand, palm up, for the dog to smell.

He sniffed at it for a while, seemed satisfied, turned around to look at his mistress, turned back to look at me, bit my outstretched hand, and then started barking again.

The young woman hurried towards us, clipped the dog onto a leash, and then glared at me. 'He doesn't usually bite!' she snapped. 'It's your backpack! He doesn't like it!'

She held her glare for a few moments, presumably waiting for me to apologize for inciting her dog to violence, and then off she marched, doubtlessly muttering to herself about how many irresponsible backpack owners one has to contend with nowadays.

Late in the afternoon, Wendy and I arrived at Far Coley Farm, just outside Little Haywood, where we had booked a very – almost worryingly – inexpensive night's bed and breakfast.

Since we had booked the cheapest possible accommodation, we were placed in a four-roomed log cabin rather than in the farmhouse itself. But since we had the cabin and its shared bathroom to ourselves, we were as happy as pigs in clover. We spent the evening, until darkness fell, sitting on the cabin's pretty little porch, looking out upon the pretty little farmyard and its pretty little duck pond, and gazing further out upon the rolling hills of the Staffordshire countryside.

The next morning, as we sat in the farmhouse conservatory enjoying a leisurely breakfast and *not* having to pack up our tent, I wondered how long the thrill of comfy beds, soft towels, cooked breakfasts, and leisurely starts would last.

The happiness I felt, by this stage of JoGLE, was of a very particular kind.

In the Book of Corinthians, in the Bible, there's a passage about love that often gets trundled out at weddings: 'Love is patient, love is kind. It does not envy, it does not boast, it is not proud. It does not dishonour others, it is not self-seeking, it is not easily angered, it keeps no record of wrongs.'

Strange as it may seem, those words capture something of the way the happiness of JoGLE felt. It wasn't a greedy, egotistical kind of happiness – or, rather, it wasn't the kind of happiness one feels when satisfying greedy, egotistical kinds of needs. And it wasn't an exciting or passionate kind of happiness. Instead, it was gentle, steady, and serene.

Readers with good memories will recall the change that came over Wendy when we left the A9 behind us and ventured forth onto the Great Glen Way.

Although I had been delighted to see that change in Wendy, it had come as no surprise, since I know she is an outdoor girl at heart, and is never more herself – that is, the best of herself – than when she is out in the wilds.

But it did surprise me, at this stage, seven hundred miles into JoGLE, to discover that the same change had taken place in *me* – someone who had previously exhibited no special fondness for the outdoors. It had taken much longer in my case, but Mother Nature had finally worked her magic. I had a new lightness in my heart and in my step.

In *The Conquest of Happiness*, Bertrand Russell says: '[W]e are creatures of Earth; our life is part of the life of the Earth, and we draw our nourishment from it just as the plants and animals do.'

He goes on to say that those pleasures that have in them no element of this contact with the Earth – gambling, for example, or, in the modern world, computer gaming or TV – are ultimately unsatisfying. The moment they cease, they leave us feeling empty and thirsty.

But, Russell continues:

> Those [pleasures] that bring us into contact with the life of the Earth have something in them profoundly satisfying; when they cease, the happiness that they have brought remains, although their intensity while they existed may have been less than that of more exciting dissipations.

And that describes my experience exactly. The pleasures of JoGLE, though rarely what you might call 'exciting', were, to me, profoundly satisfying.

From Little Haywood, we walked for three miles along the Staffordshire and Worcestershire Canal to Milford Common and the start of the Heart of England Way. Then we walked an additional fifteen miles southeast along the Way itself, first through Cannock Chase and then through farmland, to the small cathedral city of **Lichfield**.

Cannock Chase is a vast area of heathland and woodland in the county of Staffordshire, which has been designated an Area of Outstanding Natural Beauty. Crossing it, on a mid-September day, when early rain has been succeeded by mellow sunshine, I could see why.

The woodland and forest areas were fresh and green, showing only the faintest hint of autumn colouring. And the heathland, which was dominated by heather, gorse, and bracken, and embellished with a few scattered trees, had its own austere beauty. Some traces of mist hung in the air, lending both woodland and heathland an air of enchantment.

It put me strongly in mind of the forests of Merrie England. So strongly that I would scarcely have been surprised (speaking poetically, rather than literally) had I been accosted by Robin Hood and Friar Tuck, or caught a glimpse of an elfish figure scampering through the bracken, or stumbled upon a she-wolf or a wild boar.

There must be something about Cannock Chase that gives rise to such fanciful musings. Since the nineteenth century, sightings have been reported of all manner of strange creatures there: phantom cats, hellhounds, werewolves, and – most recently – a ghostly black-eyed child. Fortunately, we passed through unmolested by any such horrors, and continued merrily onwards to Lichfield.

Lichfield is, by all accounts, a splendid little city, with a magnificent three-spired medieval cathedral and lots of attractive Tudor and Georgian buildings. But, as was so often the case on JoGLE, Wendy and I saw little of it.

We arrived, early in the evening, too tired and hungry to be bothered with history and culture, and made only the very briefest detour to admire the cathedral en route to our city-centre hotel.

We had booked the cheapest room, but for some reason were given a free upgrade to an opulent room about the size of a football pitch. What with that, and with 'Fish Friday Club' at the nearby Wetherspoon's, we began to feel almost guilty about how comfortable and easy JoGLE had become.

From Lichfield, we walked eighteen miles along the Heart of England Way, and then took a three-mile detour, off the trail, to the small town of **Coleshill** where we had booked a room at a pub-hotel. As the day unfolded, I began to appreciate just how aptly the Heart of England Way is named.

For this was the England of my dreams: the England of quiet lanes and modest footpaths, of steepled churches and genial graveyards, of lush pastures politely bordered by hedges and trees, of shady woodlands vibrating with birdsong, and of slow barges on sleepy canals.

Even now, looking back on it, I feel my heart melting within me for love of England.

Throughout the day, I had those famous lines from Alfred, Lord Tennyson running through my head:

> *On either side the river lie*
> *Long fields of barley and of rye,*
> *That clothe the wold and meet the sky;*
> *And thro' the field the road runs by*
> *To many-tower'd Camelot.*

Which is weird, since we saw no river, and – as far as I know – no fields of barley and rye. But somehow those words expressed precisely what I *felt* while passing through this bit of England.

Prior to setting off on JoGLE, Wendy and I lived for five years in Vietnam. It was an exciting and exotic place to live, and, on the whole, I enjoyed being there. But sometimes I would feel a twinge of nostalgia for dear old England. And the England I conjured up in my imagination at such times was precisely *this* England.

Or, to put it another way, this was *my* England.

If you were to step, for a moment, into my England, you would find William Brown on a half-holiday, Isaac Newton sitting beneath an apple tree, Robin Hood squaring off against Little John, Mr Pickwick beaming upon the assembled members of the Pickwick Club, Lucy Pevensie stepping into a wardrobe, Marianne Dashwood walking through the wet grass at twilight, Mr Crawley walking from Hogglestock to Barchester, The Lady of Shallot making three paces through the room, and Bess, the Landlord's daughter, plaiting a dark-red love-knot into her long black hair.

This England is, I confess, a fiction. But it is an entirely *English* fiction. And it is every bit as precious to me as the real England. And the setting for this England of the imagination, which I hold so dear, looks uncannily like the Heart of England Way.

So, on that day, my heart swelled with love for England, and for the countryside, and for churches and footpaths and trees, and for rivers and streams and canals, and for Charles Dickens and Jane Austen and Anthony Trollope . . . and for JoGLE.

At one point, Wendy and I crossed a ploughed field that was so vast, and so perfectly level, and patterned with such precise furrows, and composed of such rich brown soil that I almost wept with the beauty of it all.

But it was a long, hard walk for all of that. And we weren't sorry, at the end of the day, to reach the Swan Hotel in Coleshill, where we enjoyed the less poetic pleasures of beer and a carvery dinner.

It was strange to think that there, in Coleshill, we were scarcely a mile from the eastern edge of the sprawling industrial metropolis of Birmingham.

We had arranged to stay, the following evening, with our friends Brian and Karen in the centre of the ancient market town of **Henley-in-Arden**. As luck would have it, they rent a flat there that's pretty much *on* the Heart of England Way – certainly within a dozen yards of it.

By this stage of JoGLE, we were such experienced hikers and map-readers that we could estimate with uncanny accuracy the finishing time of any day's walk, taking into account the distance, terrain, and weather conditions.

Consequently, we were able to inform Brian and Karen with smug self-confidence that we would arrive at their doorstep at some time pretty damned close to six o'clock.

The walk itself turned out to be another glorious romp through twenty-one of the greenest and pleasantest miles of England's green and pleasant land: mostly field-walking, but with a bit of woodland-, canal-, and village-walking thrown in for good measure.

At ten to six, with just half a mile to go, we were on schedule to impress the hell out of our hosts by ringing their doorbell at six o'clock *precisely*. But, as we reached the crest of a small hill at the edge of town, disaster struck.

As my right boot came down, it made contact with a slippery wet substance, and went sliding along the grass. At the same time, the unmistakeable aroma of newly passed dog-shit filled the air.

I swore and looked down. There, embedded in the nooks and crevices of my boot-tread was a cloying mass of freshly passed, mustard-coloured crap.

I swore again, and began scraping the sole of my boot back and forth across the grass. But to no avail. Almost all of the mustard-coloured dollop remained embedded in my sole.

I rubbed and scraped some more. But still to no avail. Bizarrely, the words of Jesus, from Mark 9:29, came into my mind: 'This kind can come forth by nothing, but by prayer and fasting.'

I swore again, sat down on the grass, and did the only thing that any reasonable person could have done, given the circumstances. I asked Wendy to find a twig and scrape it off.

Wendy said a few words to the effect that perhaps I ought to scrape off my own dog-shit. Fortunately, however, I was able to convince her that this would be an inefficient course of action, since it would require me to remove my boot.

If you have never scraped clingy-wet dog-shit from the tread of a hiking boot, then you can hardly appreciate what a time-consuming task it is. It kept Wendy and me (she scraping, me holding my foot nice and still) busy for an entire ten minutes.

The net result was that, instead of making a triumphant entrance at our friends' door at six o'clock precisely, we arrived ten minutes late.

Close, but no cigar.

We stayed for two nights in Henley-in-Arden, and were wined and dined royally by Brian and Karen – even to the extent of champagne on arrival.

We could happily have stayed longer. But, on JoGLE, friendship and comfort, too long indulged, become a snare. So, on the second morning, setting our faces like flint, and bidding our kind friends *adieu*, we pressed on for fourteen miles to the village of **Bidford-on-Avon**, which, as the names implies, lies on the River Avon.

It was a typical – and, hence, *glorious* – day on the Heart of England Way, which took us through woodland and pasture, through ploughed fields and fields of towering maize, and through the ancient Warwickshire town of Alcester with its enchanting Tudor cottages.

It strikes me here – and not for the first time – what a poor hand I am at this travel-writing lark. I have no eye, or ear, or heart for detail. My descriptions are always vague.

I can tell you that I walked through woodland, but I can't tell you the types of trees. I can tell you that I walked across cultivated land, but I can't tell you the types of crops. I can tell you that I climbed a crag, but I can't tell you the type of rock.

I can tell you, right now, that, at various times on the journey from John o'Groats to Land's End, I saw deer, a mole, a shrew, an otter, wild ponies, and diverse other notable fauna. But I'm damned if I can remember when and where. And I have no doubt that, had I been able to recognize them, I could have told you about a whole host of interesting birds that I spotted along the way. Ditto for flowers, shrubs, insects, and the like.

But I'm ignorant of these things. And therefore, gentle reader, so must you be.

In my defence, I should say that, while doing JoGLE, I never had any thought of writing a book about it. If I had, I'd have kept copious notes. But I hadn't. And so I didn't. And I thank my lucky stars that I didn't, because it would have *ruined* the experience.

It would have ruined the experience because it would have reduced it to something to be recorded, communicated, and ultimately sold rather than simply lived.

In C.S. Lewis's allegorical novel *The Great Divorce*, a number of departed souls, or 'Ghosts', are taken on a bus-trip from Hell to Heaven, and are given the option of staying there. One Ghost, who was a famous painter in his lifetime, takes a look at the heavenly landscape and is seized with a desire to paint it.

His guide – a former friend and fellow painter, now a Spirit – tells him that, for the present, he should forget about all of that and concentrate on *seeing*.

The Ghost is unhappy about this. He wants to get right down to painting. So the Spirit tells him, 'Why, if you are interested in the country only for the sake of painting it, you'll never learn to see the country.'

Sadly, the Ghost, who is driven by his ego, *is* interested in the country only for the sake of painting it, and decides to return to Hell rather than to endure a Heaven in which he can't display his artistic talents.

Luckily for me, I had no idea, while doing JoGLE, of writing a book about it, and was therefore spared the temptation to regard it as something to be written about rather than experienced.

The downside is that I've now had to recreate the entire journey from three imperfect sources: my memory, the route I plotted on my smartphone, and the one- or two-sentence daily updates I posted on my Facebook page.

But perhaps that isn't such a bad thing. I am, after all, not the kind of walker who cares much about naming and labelling things. Nor am I the kind of walker who likes to bother himself with too much biological, geographical, or historical detail. Instead, I'm the kind of walker who prefers to let his mind wander where it will. So I guess that this book ought to reflect that.

Anyway, Wendy and I eventually arrived at Bidford-on-Avon, where we spent the night at the Harbour Guest House, a black-and-white period building complete with beamed ceilings, log fires, and a panelled dining room.

Although it was a week since we had posted home our backpacker tent and camping paraphernalia, the thrill of staying in such comfortable surroundings hadn't yet worn off. Hadn't even begun to diminish, in fact.

I think that this was because the memory of all of those days and nights of taking down and setting up camp, and of squeezing into a tiny space, and of enduring all kinds of inconvenience and privation, remained with us. We still appreciated the *contrast*.

From Bidford-on-Avon, our plan had been to walk to the village of Chipping Camden, where the Heart of England Way connects with the northern end of the Cotswold Way.

Unfortunately, all of the accommodation at Chipping Camden was fully booked. So we were forced to re-route off the Heart of England Way, and walk fifteen miles to the village of **Dumbleton** instead.

During the morning, we followed the course of the River Avon to the market town of Evesham, and during the afternoon we improvised a route, mostly along the banks of the River Isbourne, to Dumbleton.

We spent the night at the Dumbleton Hall Hotel, a nineteenth-century manor house set in swathes of gardens and woodland, and felt very grand – but not too grand to eat pots of instant noodles in our room rather than splashing out on dinner in the restaurant.

The next day, we followed a section of the Winchcombe Way, a waymarked figure-of-eight trail centred on the town of Winchcombe, for fifteen miles to the spa town of **Cheltenham**.

Ironically, after dumping our camping equipment, we now found ourselves in the middle of an Indian summer, and enjoyed a delightful walk through lush farmland.

We arrived in Cheltenham too late, too tired, and too hungry to seek out or to care much for its Regency terraces, its celebrated pump room, its broad avenues, its fine parks, or any other of its elegancies. In fact, having settled in, we left the modest comfort of our inelegant hotel room just long enough to find an inelegant fish-and-chip shop. And that was it.

From Cheltenham, we walked three miles south to join the Cotswold Way at The Devil's Chimney: a curiously shaped limestone pillar, of uncertain origin, rising out of the ground atop Leckhampton Hill. And from there we walked fifteen miles to the village of **Painswick**.

One thing you learn very quickly on the Cotswold Way is that it's never in a hurry to get anywhere. Quite the reverse. It loops and detours and zigzags about like crazy.

Unlike many long-distance footpaths, it doesn't follow the route of old drove roads, or old Roman roads, or anything of that sort. There's nothing remotely functional about it. It just winds and wanders about, anywhere that's pleasant or interesting, and gives the impression of putting off as long as possible its arrival into Bath.

This is generally a good thing. After all, you're not there because you want to take the most efficient route from A to B. You're there to take in the scenery. But sometimes, when you're tired and footsore, or when the path takes a particularly lengthy detour so that you can walk over an especially steep hill, you wonder whether the route designers weren't just amusing themselves at your expense.

The route from The Devil's Chimney to Painswick is typical in this respect. It mooches around for a while along the top of the scarp, with fine views of open country to the right and trees to the left. Then it meanders its way through a series of woods, each one prettier than the last, before reluctantly arriving at its destination.

Painswick is a beautiful old village with an ancient church, renowned for its elegant spire and for the ninety-nine neatly clipped yew trees in its churchyard. We spent the night at St Anne's B&B, along with some American tourists who were walking the Cotswold Way.

Breakfast was a splendid affair, which included freshly baked croissants – one per person. Sadly, Wendy and I arrived at the table a tad later than our fellow guests, and therefore had to do without. But we consoled ourselves with the thought that they had gone to people who had demonstrated, by their desire to eat *ours* as well as *their own*, that they'd really, really appreciated them.

From Painswick, we walked fourteen miles along the Cotswold Way to the village of **Cam**. Our route took us over sculpted hills, through shady forests, across verdant meadows and open grassland, and through the market town of Stroud and the villages of King's Stanley and Middleyard.

We reached a point, late in the afternoon, where the Cotswold Way could have taken a direct route across level country towards the villages of Dursley and Cam. But instead it took a detour up and over Cam Long Down, a cripplingly steep hill that rises for no apparent reason out of the flattish ground to the west of the escarpment.

Local legend has it that Cam Long Down was formed from rocks tipped out from the Devil's wheelbarrow. This may or may not be true. But, either way, it is the very Devil to climb – and, I imagine, a source of diabolical delight to whoever designed the Cotswold Way.

In fairness, I have to say that, because the Cam rises so abruptly out of its surroundings, the 360-degree view from its summit is pretty damned spectacular.

Thankfully, we had a rest day to look forward to in Cam. Not that Cam itself is much to speak of. But it was delightful to lounge around in our B&B, and give our tired bodies and tender feet some much-needed recovery time.

The following day, we walked seventeen miles from Cam to **Old Sodbury** via the villages of North Nibley and Little Sodbury. A small detour would have allowed us to pass through the tiny hamlet of Waterley Bottom too, but we somehow resisted the temptation.

We also walked through the villages of Dursley and Wotton-under-Edge, which are much bigger, but less worthy of a mention because their names aren't nearly so much fun.

It was a day of woodlands and glades, of towns and villages, of scrubland and grassland, of pastures and cultivated fields, of steep-sided hills and peaceful valleys, of grazing cows and sheep, of ponds and mill streams, of hilltop monuments and ancient forts, of hedges and stone walls, of pubs and teashops, of churches and alms houses, and of cottages of honey-coloured stone.

We spent the night at the Cross Hands Hotel in Old Sodbury. It's an old posthouse, dating back to the fourteenth century, and apparently has some charming old rooms. But Wendy and I, being low-rollers, had to content ourselves with a not-quite-so-charming room in a modern part of the building.

Now that I come to think of it, though, that's not quite right. We didn't 'have to' content ourselves with a modern room. We *were* contented with it.

There may have been people at the Cross Hands Hotel staying in plusher, more stylish, more expensive rooms than ours. But what was that to us?

We had just enjoyed a long and happy walk through heart-achingly beautiful countryside. We were pleasantly tired and hungry. We had a warm room with a comfortable bed. We had a restaurant meal and cold beer to look forward to. We had leisure time to read, chat, or watch TV. And we had another long and happy walk to look forward to the following day.

We *were* contented.

In my copy of *War and Peace* – which I was still reading – I had highlighted a passage, at an earlier stage of our journey:

Pierre had learned not with his intellect but with his whole being, by life itself, that man is created for happiness, that happiness is within him, in the satisfaction of simple human needs, and that all unhappiness arises not from privation but from superfluity.

And that sums it up.

JoGLE was all about the satisfaction of 'simple human needs'. It was about staying warm and dry. It was about getting enough to eat and drink. It was about finding somewhere to sleep at night. It was about getting where you needed to be before it got dark. It was about fresh air and freedom. It was about companionship.

And being able to meet those simple human needs was enough to release the happiness within us.

Gensei, again:

> *why envy those otherworld immortals?*
> *With the happiness held in one inch-square heart*
> *you can fill the whole space between heaven and*
> *earth.*

The final nineteen-mile section of the Cotswold Way took us from Old Sodbury to **Bath**. The first six miles were flat and easy. But, after that, it was just one hill after another.

If I had to sum up my memories of that day in just one word, it would be 'green'. Apart from the last couple of urban miles, almost the entire route lies across fields. Huge, great, glorious, lush green fields.

It's heavenly country. But still, it's a tough old walk, up and down those hills. By the time we reached the outskirts of Bath, we'd had enough. But still we had to walk a couple more hilly miles, through the city, to the YHA.

Whatever mischievous soul it was that planned the tortuous route of the Cotswold Way, they outdid themselves in that final section. There's not a stone staircase, an incline, a decline, a back alley, an indirect path, or a pointless zigzag in the entire northwest corner of Bath that hasn't been drafted into service.

Admittedly, there are some fine sights along the way, including the Royal Crescent, Britain's largest and finest Regency terrace, and Bath Abbey, the last of the great medieval churches in England.

Doubtlessly, these are the official reason for all of the ups and downs and the ins and outs. But I have a strong suspicion that there's a route planner somewhere who spends his leisure hours bending over a city map, rubbing his hands and cackling in maniacal delight.

Readers who have stayed the course with me thus far won't be surprised to learn that, although Wendy and I spent a rest day in Bath, we saw nothing of it. We spent an hour or two in outdoor-gear shops, replacing our worn-out hiking boots with brand-new lightweight trail shoes. We treated ourselves to cream teas. And we lounged around in the hostel. But sightseeing wasn't on our radar.

I guess that it *would* be possible, as an End to Ender, to explore the towns and cities you pass through on your journey.

But only by building in so many rest days that you'd lose the rhythm of the walk. And that, in my opinion, would be too high a price to pay.

On JoGLE – to paraphrase Shakespeare – *the walk's the thing.*

Neither are the two arts of music and gymnastic really designed, as is often supposed, the one for the training of the soul, the other for the training of the body . . . The teachers of both have in view chiefly the improvement of the soul.

———

—**PLATO,** *REPUBLIC*

CHAPTER SEVEN

Wild Life

*Bath – Stratton-on-the-Fosse – Street –
Taunton – Sampford Peverell – Hayne – Down
St Mary – Okehampton – Stowford – Jamaica
Inn – Bodmin – Newquay*

THE PENULTIMATE STAGE OF JoGLE TOOK US 187 MILES from Bath, via Exeter, to the seaside resort of Newquay.

The route we chose was largely functional. We simply started off at Bath and walked in the general direction of Exeter; and, from there, we walked in as straight a line as possible to Newquay. We tried to navigate along footpaths and bridleways, rather than roads, wherever possible, but each day was pretty much pot-luck, as far as scenery went.

However, since the route took us through the West Country counties of Somerset, Devon, and Cornwall, famous for their lush pastures and granite moorland, pot-luck seldom disappointed.

From **Bath**, we walked thirteen miles to the village of **Stratton-on-the-Fosse**. Our route took us along minor roads, country roads, the occasional footpath, and the A367. And, although it was chosen for practical rather than aesthetic reasons, it was very pleasant nonetheless.

It was a grey early-October day. The kind of day when it's cold and damp enough to make brisk walking enjoyable, but not so cold and damp as to depress the spirits.

The pastoral landscape with its freshly ploughed fields, newly trimmed hedges, and red-, orange-, and yellow-tinged trees, was beginning to look decidedly autumnal, and, after five years of living in a tropical climate, it was a joy to behold.

In our new trail shoes, we made swift progress, and arrived at our B&B, the Kings Arms Inn, with plenty of time for R&R.

From Stratton-on-the-Fosse, we had intended to head eighteen miles southwest to the village of **Street**, near Glastonbury. But this would have meant walking a lengthy section of the wetlands area of the Somerset Levels, and a severe-weather warning, predicting widespread flooding, necessitated a change of plan. So we opted instead to take a nineteen-mile westward loop to Street, via the cathedral city of Wells.

We spent the entire day road-walking with eyes down and heads bent against the rain. So I have no clear recollection of Wells – not even of its cathedral, which is considered one of the most beautiful in England.

The part of the day I remember best was the four-mile walk along the A39 from Wells to Glastonbury. Not because it had any interest or beauty, but because it was a hazardous, footpathless slog into stinging rain and oncoming traffic.

Glastonbury, too, is just a rain-soaked blur in my memory. I recall that it had lots of boutiques catering for devotees of crystal healing, angel therapy, and Tarot reading. But little else. We stopped for coffee there, and then headed off into the rain again, for a final couple of miles, to Street.

The YHA hostel in Street is the oldest still in operation. It's a quaint little place: a Swiss-style chalet, wooden and weathered, a bit shabby in places, but with what the Japanese might call *wabi-sabi* appeal.

It's set among trees in expansive grounds at the edge of a strip of woodland, and has a secluded, back-to-nature feel about it.

During the evening, after cooking, eating, and clearing up, I sat listening to the drumming of the rain on the rooftop, and thinking how very glad I was to be there – and how very glad I was to be doing JoGLE.

JoGLE had begun principally as something that Wendy wanted to do, albeit something with enough physical challenge to tempt me a little too. But it had turned into something more. It had become a pilgrimage.

I felt that I, a sceptic and an agnostic, was beginning to understand the fascination that pilgrimage has held over the centuries for Christians, Buddhists, Muslims, Hindus, and the like.

I was beginning to understand that whatever it is you're searching for – be it peace of mind, enlightenment, redemption, inspiration, guidance, happiness, a closer walk with God, the courage to abandon your beliefs, or pretty much anything else – there are few better ways to find it than to strap on a rucksack, lace up a pair of boots, and take a couple of million steps into the unknown.

From Street, we hiked a mammoth twenty-three miles to **Taunton**, much of it across the big, beautiful – and, on this occasion, exceedingly squelchy – Somerset Levels.

It was a walk unlike any that I've ever done, across a landscape unlike any that I've ever seen: dead-flat empty grasslands, criss-crossed through with long, straight drainage ditches.

Because of the heavy rain on the previous day, there was no point even *thinking* about taking the footpath across Butleigh Moor and King's Sedge Moor, at the start of the day. So we had to walk along the small roads that zigzag through the moors instead. Even so, it was delightful to pass through such lonely, lovely country.

The Levels are home to hundreds of swans, one of which blocked our path, partway through the morning, hissing at us and beating its wings in a very aggressive manner.

I remembered reading somewhere that this is mostly bluff and bluster, and that, despite their immense size, swans really aren't that strong. Apparently, it's a myth that they can break an arm or leg with their wings. But, still, it was some time before we could summon up the courage to walk on by.

There were lots of cattle on the moors too, including a couple of eye-poppingly muscular and mean-looking bulls. Wendy and I had a long discussion, before passing one of them, about whether it was likely to swim across a drainage channel to get at us.

At around midday, we reached the village of Othery. From there, we walked southwest along minor roads to the village of North Curry, and then a final six miles, due west, to a hotel in the centre of Taunton.

The next morning, we walked southeast for nineteen miles to the Tiverton Parkway railway station. This was another cobbled-together route: first along the West Deane Way to the industrial town of Wellington, then along minor roads, and finally along the towpath of the Grand Western Canal.

As I said, it was a cobbled-together route, but still pretty bloody fantastic, on the whole, with vast expanses of verdant countryside to please the eye and soothe the spirit.

By this penultimate stage of JoGLE, walking had become as natural to me as breathing. It was what I did from nine to five each day. And it was what I *wanted to do* from nine to five each day.

I remembered, in the past, getting bored on country walks. But not any more. End to Ending had got me attuned to the rhythm, to the heartbeat, of the natural world.

End to Ending is a very different thing to day walking. On a day walk, you're a tourist, an *observer*, of nature. But, on a long-distance walk, you become *part of* nature.

It's difficult to explain without waxing poetic.

Imagine that you are out on the moors, and you see a

weathered old tree. You are acutely conscious, when you look at it, that it *belongs* there, that its roots go deep into the earth, that its branches have been bent and twisted by the wind, and that its leaves have been warmed by the sun and wetted by the rain.

If you are a day walker, you have nothing in common with that tree. *It* is a wild thing; and *you* are a tame thing. You and it have an entirely different kind of existence.

But if you have been walking for months, if week after week you have trodden the same earth, been blown by the same wind, been warmed by the same sun and wetted by the same rain, then you have a connection with it. You have a kindred existence. You belong there too.

As I said, it's difficult to explain without waxing poetic. But, however fanciful or whimsical it may sound, it's essentially true. You may not start hugging rocks and trees; you may not compose canticles to Brother Sun and Sister Moon; you may not preach to the birds and the flowers; but you really do begin to feel a connection.

This feeling of wildness was something I'd never experienced before, and it felt good.

The nineteenth-century writer, thinker, abolitionist, tax-resister, naturalist, walker and goodness-knows-what-else Henry David Thoreau was a staunch advocate of wildness.

He begins his celebrated essay *Walking* with the words:

I wish to speak a word for Nature, for absolute freedom and wildness, as contrasted with a freedom and culture merely civil – to regard man as an inhabitant, or a part and parcel of Nature, rather than a member of society.

Had I read those words pre-JoGLE, I don't suppose I would have appreciated them. Pre-JoGLE, I had never connected with the wild side of myself, and had therefore never understood its importance.

But Thoreau did. He was, in many respects, a modern-world Epicurus. He is best known today for his book *Walden*, in which he recounts a two-year experiment in natural-living in a self-made house, in a forest near the shores of Walden Pond, in Concord, Massachusetts.

Thoreau believed that wilderness and wildness are essential to human flourishing, that they are indispensable sources of invigoration, inspiration, and strength. 'From the forest and wilderness,' he said, 'come the tonics and barks which brace mankind.'

And this was precisely my experience on JoGLE. It took me a while to get into it. But, by the third and final month, wildness and wilderness had worked its magic upon me. I really was invigorated, inspired, and strengthened.

Thoreau famously observed that 'The mass of men lead lives of quiet desperation'. In my humdrum, everyday life, I identified with that. But, on JoGLE, I could no longer be numbered among the mass of men. I was fully engaged. Fully alive.

Although Wendy and I hadn't realized it when we set off from Taunton, the Tiverton Parkway railway station isn't actually *in* the town of Tiverton. It's located seven miles east of it, close by the village of **Sampford Peverell**.

Had we not stopped for a beer at a pub in Sampford Peverell, and got talking to the barman, we wouldn't have discovered our mistake until we reached Tiverton – which would have been seven miles too late.

From Tiverton Parkway, we caught a train to Exeter, where we spent two nights with our friend Hilary, who has an apartment close to the historic quayside on the River Exe.

As was the case whenever we broke our journey to stay with friends, we were fed, watered, and pampered quite royally. Hilary even moved into her spare bedroom, alongside her cat Hobbes, so that we could luxuriate in her big comfy bed.

From Sampford Peverell, we hiked fourteen miles in a westerly direction to the tiny hamlet of **Hayne**.

The morning's walk was a flat and easy stroll along the winding course of the Grand Western Canal, to the town of Tiverton. And the afternoon's walk took us up and over lots of small hills, across farmland.

I have a vivid memory, from that afternoon, of walking along a grassy path through gently rolling pasture, and being struck by how outrageously *alive* everything was.

The grass at my feet was long and lush, and gave the impression of having triumphed gleefully over every attempt to cut it back or trample it down. The bushes and ferns at the side of the path were so thriving and dense that they seemed to be trying to fill every cubic inch of space with as much organic matter as possible. The rich pastureland, the fields of freshly ploughed earth, and the trees and bushes surrounding them were equally bursting with life.

And so was I.

As I walked the final few miles towards the farmhouse B&B at Hayne where we were to spend the night, I found myself unconsciously humming the tune of the Elvis Presley song 'Wild in the Country', and realized that it expressed exactly how I felt.

By this stage of JoGLE, I had come to feel – and I mean this literally, not just poetically – part of the Earth.

From Hayne, the next morning, we continued west for twelve miles: first to the village of Morchard Bishop, and then along a section of the Two Moors Way walking trail to a B&B in the village of **Down St Mary**.

This was another day of pastures and ploughed fields, of hedges and trees, of cows, horses, and sheep, and of quintessentially English villages.

Somewhere along the route, we stopped at a pub. Wendy took a photo of me, standing before an open fire with a pint of beer in my hand, and I was startled to see how much my appearance had changed. I had gone from podgy and soft to slim and toned in just twelve weeks.

It was a whole other me; a better me; a healthier, happier, more balanced me.

There's a passage in Plato's *Republic* where the main character, Socrates, discusses the value of physical exercise with a young man named Glaucon:

> 'Have you noticed how a lifelong devotion to physical exercise, to the exclusion of anything else, produces a certain type of mind? Just as a neglect of it produces another type? One type tends to be tough and uncivilised, the other soft and oversensitive.'

Glaucon replies:

> 'Yes, I have noticed that excessive emphasis on athletics produces a pretty uncivilised type, while a purely literary and academic training leaves a man with less backbone than is decent.'

Looking at that photo, I felt, for the first time in years, that I'd got the balance right.

My body looked lithe, limber, and ready for action. My mind (that is, my intellect) felt the same. And I realized that this proper balance of the physical and mental was, in no small degree, accountable for my more robust, positive, and engaged emotional state.

Plato believed that we humans have a dual nature, that we are bodies and minds. And he believed that we can only reach our potential – we can only become the best of ourselves – when our two natures are, as it were, pulling together.

To the modern mind, Plato's ideas often seem fanciful and idealistic. But, in this instance, he spoke from experience.

When we think of Plato, the image that generally springs to mind is that of a be-robed, balding, soft-bearded old man – the ultimate other-worldly intellectual. But that's quite misleading. In fact, he was known for his imposing physique, and was so skilled a wrestler that he is said to have competed at the prestigious Isthmian Games.

Indeed, the name 'Plato' (from the Greek *platon*, meaning 'broad') is said to have been given to him by his wrestling coach on account of his powerful shoulders. His birth name was Aristocles.

Plato had learned, from experience, that physical vigour promotes intellectual vigour, and that the two together promote psychological vigour.

And now I had learned it too. My sitting-still-and-brooding-self had been, in Plato's words, 'soft and oversensitive'. But my constantly-in-motion self . . . well, he was a whole other guy.

From Down St Mary, Wendy and I walked seventeen miles southwest to the town of **Okehampton**.

For most of the way, we followed a section of the Devonshire Heartland Way: a forty-three-mile walking trail that runs between Okehampton and the village of Stoke Canon. This took us mostly along footpaths and bridleways through undulating farmland.

Partway through the afternoon, we clocked up our thousandth JoGLE mile. But this was more a cause for sadness than celebration – an unwelcome reminder that our journey was nearing its end.

We spent the night at the YHA in Okehampton, a converted railway-goods shed on the edge of Dartmoor, and then set off early to the tiny village of **Stowford**.

The first half of our fourteen-mile walk to Stowford took us southwest along the Granite Way: a traffic-free cycleway that runs along the edge of Dartmoor, between Okehampton and the village of Lydford.

The Granite Way is full of interest, offering views of Okehampton Castle, Meldon Lake, and, on its left-hand side, the Dartmoor National Park with its wild, empty moors, exposed granite hilltops, and herds of semi-feral Dartmoor ponies.

Best of all, at one point it crosses the West Okement River by means of the Meldon Viaduct, a wrought-iron railway bridge that towers spectacularly above the river and the canopy of the surrounding trees.

The second half of our journey from Okehampton took us west through farmland and small villages to some splendidly rural B&B accommodation at Townleigh Farm, near Stowford.

From Townleigh Farm, we walked twenty-one miles to the remote(ish) **Jamaica Inn**, on Bodmin Moor.

I say 'remote(ish)', because, although it's slap-bang in the middle of the moor, there's a tiny hamlet, Bolventor, plus a clonking-great A-road, the A30, nearby.

The greater part of the day's journey was a pleasant but unremarkable hike along minor roads and footpaths through rural Devon. The last few miles, though, across the empty, heather-clad granite moorland of Bodmin Moor, were something special. Like Thoreau, I find that my spirits 'infallibly rise' when I am surrounded by bleakness and wilderness. And the same goes for Wendy. So we both arrived at Jamaica Inn in good spirits.

Jamaica Inn, a former coaching inn, built in 1750, provided both the setting and the title for Daphne du Maurier's 1936 novel, set in the harsh and violent world of Cornish smugglers and wreckers in the early nineteenth century.

Her inspiration for the novel came to her while staying at the inn, after getting lost in the mist while horse-riding on Bodmin Moor. That would be a very easy thing to do. Wendy and I crossed it on a bright autumn day. But even so, without the GPS on my trusty smartphone, navigating it would have been no easy matter.

Today, Jamaica Inn is a hotel/pub/restaurant/museum that trades quite shamelessly upon its literary and lawless associations, with olde-worlde décor and abundant references to du Maurier's novel and the world of smuggling. It is also (and I say this with a world-weary sigh) reputed to be one of the most haunted places in Britain.

But, for all that, it's a fun and comfortable place to stay – especially at the end of a long hike.

From Jamaica Inn, we walked fifteen miles to the town of **Bodmin**.

We spent the morning heading south along the eastern side of Colliford Lake, Cornwall's second-largest lake. It was a splendid walk across the moor. Not quite as splendid as the previous afternoon's walk, since our path lay along a minor road rather than along footpaths and bare moorland. But splendid nonetheless.

I can't remember details. I have a general recollection of a wide expanse of water on our right, and of scrubby grassland, meagre trees, and herds of Dartmoor ponies on our left. But I recall very clearly that I enjoyed it immensely.

At one point in his classic work of philosophical fiction *Zen and the Art of Motorcycle Maintenance*, Robert Pirsig talks about the kinds of things that one 'should notice' when walking up a mountain: 'This leaf has jagged edges. This rock looks loose. From this place the snow is less visible, even though closer.'

I wouldn't, for a moment, dispute the value, to Pirsig and others, of this kind of observant awareness. But such conscious attention to detail isn't at all my cup of tea.

Once or twice, in the past, I've tried to walk 'mindfully', to focus my attention on 'this leaf', or 'this rock', or the coolness of the breeze, or the singing of the birds. But it distracts and annoys me. My attention gets focused not on the intended objects, but on my own attempts to focus.

I find it far more rewarding to practise *un*-mindfulness: to climb a mountain, or to cross a moor, or to paddle in the ocean, or to lie beneath the stars without making the slightest effort to notice or focus upon anything.

I get my kicks by *absorbing* rather than *observing*.

This makes me, I think, what C.S. Lewis, in the second chapter of his book *The Four Loves*, calls a 'nature-lover'.

Nature-lovers, as Lewis uses the term, are not the kind of people who seek out the beauty of individual natural objects such as rocks, streams, and flowers. Neither are they the kind of people who take special delight in beautiful vistas.

In fact, Lewis says, there's nothing so irritating for the true nature-lover as sharing a ramble with a botanist or a landscape painter. The botanist will insist on pointing out beautiful objects, and the landscape painter will insist on pointing out beautiful views.

Nature-lovers find all of this annoying. They're not interested in particulars. They want to experience the whole.

Lewis writes:

Nature-lovers want to receive as fully as possible whatever nature, at each particular time and place, is, so to speak, saying. The obvious richness, grace and harmony of some scenes are no more precious to them than the grimness, bleakness, terror, monotony, or 'visionary dreariness' of others. The featurelessness itself gets from them a willing response. It is one more word uttered by nature.

He considers the English Romantic poet William Wordsworth to be the archetypal nature-lover.

Wordsworth decried 'giving way to a comparison of scene with scene', being 'bent overmuch on superficial things', and 'pampering' oneself 'with meagre novelties of colour and proportion'. It was far better, he thought, to be sensible to 'the moods of time or season', and to 'the affections and spirit' of a place.

This describes my attitude to nature, and to the countryside, to a 'T'. So I have no hesitation in describing myself as a nature-lover. I hadn't realized it before setting off on JoGLE. And it took me a long time to realize it *while doing* JoGLE. But, none-theless, a nature-lover I am.

After crossing Bodmin Moor, we walked southwest, along minor roads and the occasional footpath, to Bodmin.

Bodmin is one of Cornwall's major towns. But, despite spending an entire rest day there, I remember almost nothing about it.

I remember that Wendy and I stayed in an unpretentious but adequately comfortable room at a Thai restaurant/hotel in the centre of town. And I remember that, on our first night there, we lounged on the bed, ate crisps and chocolate, and watched *Strictly Come Dancing*. But, apart from that, it's all a blank.

Our journey from Bodmin to **Newquay** – the final part of the penultimate section of JoGLE – took us twenty miles west, along minor roads, through gently undulating farmland.

Summing it up, like that, it all sounds a little dull. Or, at any rate, of little consequence. And if you asked me about it, and understood how little of it I can actually recall, you'd think that it really *was* of little consequence.

But that's not how it was. And that's not how it is.

I have two photographs in front of me now, which I took that day using my smartphone.

The first shows a leaf-strewn forest path, which is enclosed overhead by the canopy of the trees, giving it the appearance of a tunnel. The second shows a broad pasture extending to a line of trees at the horizon, with white cotton-wool clouds in a pale-blue sky overhead.

Without those photographs, I might struggle to remember those scenes. But, at the time, they were magical. And, even now, something of their magic remains.

In the spring of 1802, my fellow nature-lover William Wordsworth came across a long belt of daffodils while walking with his sister Dorothy in the Lake District.

This event inspired him, a couple of years later, to pen his most famous poem, commonly known as 'Daffodils', which begins:

> *I wandered lonely as a cloud*
> *That floats on high o'er vales and hills,*
> *When all at once I saw a crowd,*
> *A host of golden daffodils;*
> *Beside the lake, beneath the trees,*
> *Fluttering and dancing in the breeze.*

The poem, though, isn't just about that one experience, that fleeting moment in time. It's also about memory, and how memory can make such fleeting moments last.

The poem ends:

> *I gazed – and gazed – but little thought*
> *What wealth the show to me had brought:*

> *For oft, when on my couch I lie*
> *In vacant or in pensive mood,*
> *They flash upon that inward eye*
> *Which is the bliss of solitude;*
> *And then my heart with pleasure fills,*
> *And dances with the daffodils.*

And it's the same for me with that forest path and that broad pasture. I may struggle to remember precisely when and where I saw them. I may confuse them with similar paths and similar pastures. But nonetheless their beauty remains. As does the beauty of a thousand other half-remembered scenes.

At the time, I 'little thought what wealth to me the show had brought'. But now, when I look back – even after all this time – 'my heart with pleasure fills'.

We arrived at our destination, a neat little B&B in Newquay, early in the evening.

Newquay is a major tourist destination, principally on account of its long sandy beaches, especially Fistral Beach, which is a Mecca for surfers. And, like many popular seaside towns, it's bursting with clubs, pubs, bars, cafés, and amusement arcades.

Normally, I quite like busy seaside resorts. And, although I'm not one for clubs and bars, I'm as likely as the next man to stuff myself with hot donuts and to pour money into a slot-machine.

But, after spending so much time in the countryside, I found it all a bit tawdry and depressing. Well, not *depressing*, exactly. But I can't say that I liked it much.

That night, Wendy and I sat in a very cheap and very cheerful fish-and-chip shop, and looked forward, with as much sadness as anticipation, to the final section of our End to End adventure.

The end of a melody is not its goal: but nonetheless, had the melody not reached its end it would not have reached its goal either. A parable.

———————

—FRIEDRICH NIETZSCHE

CHAPTER EIGHT

Bittersweet

Newquay – Perranporth – Portreath –
St Ives – Pendeen – Land's End

FOR WENDY AND ME, THE CONTRAST BETWEEN HOW JoGLE began and how it ended could hardly have been greater.

It started with a 120-mile trudge from John o'Groats to Inverness: a road-walk of such epic dullness that no right-minded person would ever undertake it except as a means to an end. It ended with a seventy-mile hike from Newquay to Land's End: a coastal hike of such constant yet varied beauty that no right-minded person would ever want it to end.

For this final part of our journey, we followed a short – alas, all too short – section of the South West Coast Path.

The SWCP, in its entirety, stretches 630 miles from Minehead, in Somerset, to Poole Harbour, in Dorset, encompassing the whole of the Cornwall and Devon coasts. Its origins date back to the nineteenth century when coastguards patrolled the cliff-tops of the southwest coast, scanning the bays and inlets for evidence of smuggling. Today, it's the longest and most popular long-distance footpath in Britain.

The remarkable thing about the SWCP is that for almost its entire length it passes seamlessly from one scenic splendour to the next, and the next, and the next.

At any given moment, you may be navigating along the edge of a cliff, looking down upon the breakers crashing into the rocks below, or traversing a stretch of sandy beach, gazing out across an expanse of turquoise sea. Later, you may pass a remote lighthouse perched on the farthest edge of a grassy headland. And shortly after that, you may be clambering down the steep side of a rocky inlet.

At each stage, you say to yourself that this can't possibly last, that sooner or later all of this grandeur and beauty must give way to something less inspiring. But it doesn't. Each twist and turn of the trail brings fresh delights.

The gods were smiling upon us as we started out from **Newquay**. We had always expected that by this stage of our journey we would be battling with autumn winds and wet and cold. But instead we found ourselves bathed in the warm sunshine of an Indian summer.

The thirteen-mile stretch of coastal path from Newquay to the seaside town of **Perranporth** is categorized as challenging. But we were now so fit and lean, and so used to carrying our backpacks, that it felt like a mere stroll in the park.

About two miles from Perranporth, the SWCP winds its way across Penhale Sands, an area of grass-, moss-, and lichen-covered dunes to the rear of Perran Beach. The route is waymarked, but the waymarks are so often hidden by the dunes that they're difficult to follow. So we abandoned the 'path' and walked along the beach instead.

Perran Beach is wide and sandy and spectacular. It overlooks Perran Bay and the Atlantic Ocean to the east, and is backed by Penhale Sands to the west. At its southern end, close to Perranporth, the dunes give way to cliffs, arches, and stacks.

As I walked along, enjoying the autumn sunshine and the gentle breeze blowing in from the sea, my thoughts wandered back twenty years to one of the best days of my life. Wendy and I were travelling around Australia at the time, and were camping by the sea, a few miles from St Kilda, a suburb of Melbourne.

We had nothing planned for the day. So Wendy decided to hang around the campsite and catch up on some personal chores while I opted to take a walk along the beach.

I was in no hurry. I had nothing to do, and all day to do it. So, rather than taking a slow, lazy saunter along the sand, I decided to take an even slower, lazier paddle in the sea. I splashed, ankle-deep in the balmy waters of Port Phillip Bay all the way to St Kilda. Then I turned around and splashed my way home again.

My memories of that day are hazy. I recall sunshine, blue sky, warm water, and lapping waves, but nothing more specific. I can't recall what I thought about as I walked, either. All I know is that my thoughts wandered freely and pleasantly.

It has often struck me as curious that a day like that, with no excitement or stimulation, and with nothing achieved and nothing gained, should stand out in my memory as among the happiest I have known. What was it, I have often wondered, that made it so special?

In the 'Fifth Walk' of *Reveries of a Solitary Walker*, Rousseau asks himself the same question as he looks back upon the happiest period of his own life: two idle months he spent on the Island of Saint-Pierre, on Lake Bienne, in Switzerland.

He passed his time there indulging his interest in botany, watching the labourers working at the harvest, and – sweetest of all – taking a small boat out onto the lake.

Of this last activity – or rather, non-activity – he says:

> [T]here, stretching out full-length in the boat and turning my eyes skyward, I let myself float and drift wherever the water took me, often for several hours on end, plunged in a host of vague yet delightful reveries, which though they had no distinct or permanent subject, were still in my eyes infinitely to be preferred to all that I had found most sweet in the so-called pleasures of life.

At evening time, Rousseau would often return to the lake shore and sit on the shingle in some secluded spot.

> [T]here the noise of the waves and the movement of the water, taking hold of my senses and driving all other agitation from my soul, would plunge it into a delicious reverie . . . and it was enough to make me pleasurably aware of my existence, without troubling myself with thought.

Here, in describing the blissful hours he spent at Lake Bienne, Rousseau identifies precisely what it was that had made the hours I spent on that Australian beach so blissfully and unforgettably sweet. Namely, the experience – which most of us seldom get to enjoy – of *simply being*.

In our everyday lives, our thoughts, affections, and desires are continually being dragged away from the here and now to some other place, some other time, or some other possible state of affairs. We are forever plotting, analysing, regretting, longing, grasping, or clinging. Seldom just living.

But that day, on that Australian beach, those thoughts were quieted. I was ten thousand miles away from the cares and concerns of my everyday life. The past and the future were sufficiently remote to have lost their accustomed influence upon me. And so the present moment – the lapping of the waves, the warmth of the sun and the blue of the sky – was everything.

At St Kilda, I enjoyed this blissful state for just a few hours. But on Lake Bienne, Rousseau experienced it, day after day, for weeks. And the longer it continued, the more captivating it became, until eventually he came to regard it as 'the height of happiness'.

As we walked along Perran Beach, that autumn day, with our End to End adventure fast drawing to a close, a thought struck me with such sudden force that I had to stop for a moment to let it sink in. *JoGLE was my Saint-Pierre!*

All of those slow miles through towns, villages, farmland, and forests, all of those slow miles over moors, mountains, and hills, all of those slow miles across beaches, ploughed fields, and pastures, all of those slow miles beside lakes, rivers, and streams, all of those slow miles had brought me, little by little, to a very special state of mind.

It was the same state of mind that Rousseau experienced at St Pierre, and which he describes so lyrically and so beautifully as:

> a state where the soul can find a resting-place secure enough to establish itself and concentrate its entire being there, with no need to remember the past or reach into the future, where time is nothing to it, where the present runs on indefinitely but this duration goes unnoticed, with no sign of the passing of time, and no other feeling of deprivation or enjoyment, pleasure or pain, desire or fear than the simple feeling of existence, a feeling that fills our soul entirely, as long as this state lasts[.]

Wendy and I arrived at Perranporth at around four o'clock. It's a resort town, and popular with surfers, but, unlike its bigger, brasher neighbour, Newquay, it's neat, tidy, and unspoiled.

We treated ourselves to ice-creams and sat on a rock on the beach to eat them. It was a perfect afternoon. We were surrounded on every side by the freshest, cleanest shades of blue, green, and turquoise. The wide expanse of sea, the even wider expanse of sky, and the grassy headlands complemented one another so perfectly, and evoked such a sense of peace, freedom, and contentment, that they might have been put together for that very purpose by some Cosmic Designer.

Perranporth YHA is situated south of the town, perched upon a grassy cliff-top overlooking Perran Bay and the Atlantic Ocean. It's compact, basic, and perhaps even a little shabby, but it's also comfortable and welcoming.

We spent a deliciously long evening there, sitting in cosy chairs by the window, looking back upon the long and happy journey that had brought us to Perranporth from John o'Groats, and looking ahead to the short journey that would bring us, all too quickly, to Land's End.

Our thirteen-mile hike from Perranporth to the YHA at **Portreath** began in dramatic fashion with a winding cliff-top walk, through gorse and heather, and past chimneys, disused mineshafts, and other relics of the Cornish tin-mining industry. After that, the path continued to twist and turn along the contour of the cliff, so that the view constantly shifted between sea and land and shoreline.

By this time, with the end of our three-month journey fast approaching, each walk was something to be savoured. We were conscious that these glorious Indian-summer days, these days of fresh air and freedom, these days of *dolce far niente* (literally, 'sweet doing nothing'), would soon be over.

As we were now very fit and well adapted to the rigours of the walk, we found ourselves eating up the trail on the SWCP at immense speed.

In the early days of JoGLE, on the road to Inverness, we had naturally adopted a slow, plodding style of walking. But, as the weeks and months had progressed, our walking style had evolved into something so fast and efficient that it bordered on a jog.

This is a very pleasant way to move. It gets the lungs working and the heart beating, and it makes you feel full of energy and full of life. But it can also make a modest-distance walk feel disappointingly short.

So, to make the final stages of JoGLE last as long as possible, we included plenty of stops. On this day, we stopped for beers at Trevaunance Cove, stopped for ice-creams at Chapel Porth, and stopped to enjoy the sunshine on numerous benches, beaches, and boulders en route. Even so, the miles flew by.

Before we knew it, we had left behind the flowering heather and gorse, the narrow paths winding prettily across undulating moorland, the granite cliffs and grassy slopes, the steep-sided rocky inlets, and the gentle breakers scudding across the surface of sandy beaches.

We arrived, late in the afternoon, at the fishing village of Portreath, and from there took a mile-and-a-half detour off the SWCP to Portreath YHA, a converted barn in the grounds of a working farm.

As it was midweek and late in the season, we had the hostel to ourselves. During the long evening, our thoughts and conversation returned, again and again, to the same theme: the nearness of our journey's end.

It was strange, now, for me to think back to the first stage of JoGLE, when each day's walk had seemed too long and too hard, and when Land's End couldn't come soon enough for my liking.

I never imagined, back then, that the time would come when the days' walks would seem too short and almost too easy, and when Land's End would seem to be approaching all too fast.

Back then, I had regarded JoGLE as a challenge to be completed, an obstacle to be overcome. I little thought that the time would come when I would think of it not as a means to an end but as an end in itself, not as an obstacle to be overcome but as an experience to be savoured.

I never dreamed that I would come to regard it – to use Rousseau's phrase – as 'the height of happiness'.

The following day, we enjoyed another unseasonably warm and sunny hike along another magnificent stretch of the South West Coast Path. This time, our route ran seventeen miles from Portreath to the popular holiday resort of **St Ives**.

For the first five or six miles, the path wove in and out of small headlands, and past coves, stacks, and islands with splendid names such as Ralph's Cupboard, Deadman's Cove, and Hell's Mouth.

This cliff-top-hugging section ended at Godrevy Head, a

large square promontory overlooking Godrevy Island with its lighthouse, which is said to have been the inspiration for Virginia Woolf's novel *To the Lighthouse*.

From there, the path headed southwest across sand dunes to the mouth of the River Hayle, and then took a long, almost circular, detour around the muddy flats of the Hayle estuary before heading northwest into St Ives.

The detour around the estuary contributed about four miles to our day's tally. These were welcome extra miles, since by now we were keen to prolong each walk and hold on, for as long as we reasonably could, to our JoGLE experience.

But, despite the detours and the tea-stops and the view-stops, I was acutely conscious that our journey was drawing swiftly and inexorably to a close, that only two days' walking remained.

It was a sad thought. But it was a sadness tinged with sweetness.

I remember once, at that period of my life when I was slowly but systematically dismantling my Christian faith, falling asleep on my bed while listening to a Sting CD.

It just so happened – quite by chance, no doubt – that the song 'Fragile' was playing as I entered that strange region of consciousness halfway between waking and sleeping. And in that altered state of perception something peculiar and wonderful happened.

When the song entered the musical interlude, Sting's

classical guitar, which carries the solo, spoke to me. It didn't speak to me in words. There could be no translation. But it spoke to me as clearly as words ever could about the fragility of life.

It told me – as far as words can express it – that life is brief, that it is over almost as soon as it is begun, that it fades away as swiftly and surely as the bloom of a rose, but that it is all the more beautiful for all of that.

The experience was remarkable in itself. But even more so because the insight it contained went so much against the grain of my conscious thinking at that time.

I had just, very reluctantly, begun to abandon my belief in everlasting life, and, with it, my belief in there being anything of lasting meaning in life.

I found this terribly depressing. If life had no lasting meaning, then what was the point of it? What was the point of *anything*? Of what use was it to experience beauty or pleasure or love, knowing that none of these things would endure?

I felt disappointed and angry with life, with the universe, with everything.

But somehow, the notes and phrases from Sting's guitar solo opened my mind to a new idea: to the idea that life and beauty and pleasure and love are all the more precious precisely *because* they cannot last.

This was an idea that my conscious, analytical mind, in its hurt and bruised state, would have rejected angrily. But in that semi-conscious state, it sneaked in under the radar, lodged itself inside me, and made its presence felt.

The Japanese have a phrase, *mono no aware*, that captures this idea beautifully. Literally, it translates as 'the pathos of things', and it refers to the awareness of the impermanence of things – an awareness that, though sad, is tinged with beauty.

This state of awareness arises when you are confronted with something beautiful, and at the same time confronted with its transience. The feelings of joy and sadness that are evoked by this double consciousness merge together into a new and profound emotion.

The Japanese tradition of *hanami*, cherry blossom viewing, provides a perfect illustration of *mono no aware*.

There are lots of varieties of cherry tree in Japan, many of which bloom for just a few days, each spring. Every year, the Japanese hold *hanami* parties beneath the flowering trees to enjoy the beauty of the blossoms, and the intensity of the experience is heightened by the knowledge that this beauty is short-lived.

Intrinsically, there is perhaps no more beauty in cherry blossom than there is in apple or pear blossom. But the transience of cherry blossom evokes a feeling that goes beyond the ordinary appreciation of beauty. It evokes – or *can* evoke in a sensitive observer – the inexpressibly sad, sweet, and tender feeling of *mono no aware*.

At St Ives, we were just twenty-five miles – a single day's walk, at a push – from Land's End. Our plan, though, was to do the journey in two stages: first, fifteen miles from St Ives to the village of Pendeen, and then ten miles from Pendeen to Land's End. But before that, we took an unprecedented two days' rest in St Ives.

Not that two lean, mean walking-machines like Wendy and I needed that amount of rest. But we had previously arranged to meet a friend in Pendeen, and were running ahead of schedule. Plus, we were not at all averse to delaying, for a couple of days, our arrival at Land's End.

St Ives was a splendid place to kick back and contemplate the end of JoGLE.

It's a pretty little seaside resort with four beautiful sandy beaches. The older part of town, near to the shoreline, is a pleasing mishmash of narrow, uneven streets lined with old-fashioned houses and shops. And just as importantly, for cash-strapped, calorie-deprived, long-distance walkers, the newer part of town has a Wetherspoon's.

We stayed at the Trelhoyan Manor Hotel, a nineteenth-century mansion set in lovely gardens overlooking St Ives Bay. This is run by the Christian Guild, a Christian holiday and hotel company that provides 'Christian-based holidays for everyone who is a Christian, who is seeking to find Christ, or who is in sympathy with the Christian faith'. And, although neither Wendy nor I fulfil any of those criteria, we had a pleasant stay nonetheless.

Although it was past the middle of October, the Indian summer continued unabated. It wasn't quite the same as a regular summer though. It was just as warm and pleasant, but the colours were different. Less vibrant.

This meant that the wide expanse of sand at St Ives Bay was

straw-coloured rather than golden, the sea was viridian rather than turquoise, and the sky was powder blue rather than azure. But these more subdued colours complemented our wistful End-of-JoGLE mood perfectly.

By this time, both Wendy and I felt that we could happily have carried on walking indefinitely, that we could have continued along the South West Coast Path, past Land's End, all the way to Poole Harbour – and then on to who-knows-where.

But that wasn't possible. JoGLE, like all good things, had to come to an end. We had livings to earn.

For me, the thought that JoGLE would soon end wasn't entirely negative. In fact, it had a very positive aspect. It heightened the experience of those final few days, made me feel as though every minute counted, and made End to End as a whole seem all the more precious.

In *Essays in Idleness*, one of the great works of medieval Japanese literature, the Buddhist monk Yoshida Kenkō says:

> If man were never to fade away like the dews of Adashino, never to vanish like the smoke over Toribeyama, how things would lose their power to move us! The most precious thing in life is its uncertainty.

This is pretty much the message that Sting's classical guitar had tried to teach me all those years ago. And it was a message that JoGLE was now reinforcing.

JoGLE was soon to end. And that was sad. But the knowledge that it must end soon was precisely what gave it much of its 'power to move us'.

Mono no aware.

On the very first stage of JoGLE, it occurred to me that our journey could be seen as a microcosm of human life in its constant switching back and forth between hardship and comfort, toil and repose, pain and pleasure. Now, as our journey drew to a close, I realized that it could also be seen as a symbol of human life in respect of its impermanence.

We knew, from the very first step, that JoGLE wouldn't last, that it would consist of a series of moments, both good and bad, with a beginning and an end. And this knowledge added to the poignancy of those moments.

In the same way, life consists of a series of moments, both good and bad, with a beginning and an end. And, if we are wise, we will let this knowledge add poignancy to those moments. We will see not only the inescapability but also the beauty of impermanence.

Our penultimate day's walk on the South West Coast Path, from St Ives to **Pendeen**, was one of the toughest and most rewarding of the whole of JoGLE. The path hugged the coastline for the entire fifteen miles, with frequent ascents and descents between high cliff-tops and secluded coves. And just to make things more challenging, we had to battle against a stiff wind for most of the day.

The cliff-top sections are very exposed in parts, and at one point we had to abandon the SWCP and walk further inland, rather than risk being blown over the edge.

It's a stunning piece of coastline though, wild and rugged, rocky and remote, and worth every step.

Towards the end of the afternoon, about four miles from Pendeen, we took a brief detour off the path and met up with our friend Karen (not the Brian-and-Karen Karen) at a car park near the tiny hamlet of Rosemergy.

After exchanging greetings, we all marched off together in great high spirits, in the direction of Pendeen. It was only when Karen stopped, gasping for breath, after keeping pace with us for just a few minutes that we realized how freakishly fit and fast we had become.

We spent the night – our last one on the trail – at a B&B in the village of Pendeen. We ate dinner at a nearby pub, and there, over curry and beer, Karen arranged to meet us (with celebratory champagne, bless her) the following afternoon at the iconic Land's End signpost.

On the final day of JoGLE, the blue skies and sunshine were replaced by grey cloud, mist, and rain. The Indian summer was ended.

The ten-mile walk along the South West Coast Path from Pendeen to **Land's End** is magnificent whatever the weather though. So there was no sense of disappointment or anti-climax or let-down. Things were just different, that's all.

The path, here, winds along the edge of the cliff-tops, twist-ing and turning into every little nook and cranny as if to make the journey to Land's End last as long as possible.

The first hour of the walk took us through one of Cornwall's oldest mining districts, past the remnants of the Levant Mine, from which tin and copper ores were once raised, and past the relics of two engine houses from the Crown Mine, perched partway down the cliffs near Botallack head.

The path then took us to Cape Cornwall, a small headland from which, on a clearer day, we might have caught our first sight of Land's End. From there, we walked along the cliff edge to Aire Point, the northern tip of the mile-long surfing beach of Whitesand Bay, with some treacherous clambering up and down rocks to keep things interesting.

Land's End, with its rocky headland descending towards the sea and petering out into a series of tiny islets, is easily recogniz-able from a distance. As we headed down from Aire Point, onto the dunes behind Whitesand Bay, it came into view.

It had been our destination and goal for three months, for eleven hundred and fifty miles, and for two-and-a-half million steps. And now, at last, surrounded by a grey choppy sea and thinly veiled by mist, there it was.

There had been times on our long journey when I had thought that this sight could never come soon enough, when I had imagined that walking this final mile would be a blessed relief. But looking at it now, the feeling was neither joy nor relief, nor even a sense of achievement. It was sadness.

A poem by the Japanese poet Bashō, a Zen Buddhist, reputed to be the greatest master of the Haiku, came into my mind:

> *Even in Kyōto –*
> *Hearing the cuckoo's cry –*
> *I long for Kyōto.*

As a Buddhist, Bashō understood that there is an element of suffering even in life's most pleasant experiences, that all earthly joys are fading and impermanent.

There is sadness in gazing at a cherry blossom, knowing that its beauty must soon fade. There is sadness in watching children at play, knowing that their innocent joys must eventually give way to adult cares. There is sadness in loving a woman or a man, knowing that we cannot hold onto them forever.

Sadness of this kind permeates every part of life. Even the most supreme joys contain the seeds of sorrow, because they cannot last.

So, even as Bashō hears the cuckoo's cry in his beloved Kyoto, he is conscious of a sense of longing. His joy is tempered by the knowledge that he cannot hold onto the moment, that he cannot possess Kyoto forever.

And yet there is sweetness in his sorrow.

Just as the fragility of a cherry blossom enhances its beauty, and just as the brevity of childhood makes it all the more precious, and just as the impermanence of love adds to its intensity, Bashō's understanding that he cannot hold onto the moment makes the moment all the more poignant.

I realized – even as I felt my throat constrict and the tears begin to well up in my eyes – that this was precisely how JoGLE should end.

I turned to Wendy. 'It makes you want to cry, doesn't it?'

She nodded.

We hitched up our rucksacks, one last time, and strode out, for one last mile, towards Land's End.

Epilogue

IT'S A CRISP OCTOBER AFTERNOON. WENDY AND I HAVE finished JoGLE, have spent a few nights with Karen and her parents, in Devon, and are now travelling by train to Runcorn in Cheshire.

Normal life is just a few hours away.

I gaze out of the window at the surrounding countryside. There are freshly ploughed fields in the foreground, and trees and hills in various shades of green in the background.

A wave of nostalgia washes over me.

Not so very long ago, I viewed ploughed fields as mere inconveniences: muddy, slow-going, and difficult to navigate. But now I feel that nothing – really, *nothing* – would give me greater pleasure than to cross those ploughed fields and disappear into those green trees and hills.

Kierkegaard famously said, 'Life can only be understood backwards; but it must be lived forwards.'

As far as life as a whole goes, I can't say I agree. I don't understand life backwards any more than I understood it forwards. But when I look back on JoGLE – at that small but significant slice of my life – his words ring true.

I lived JoGLE forwards, and I misunderstood it. I thought that the sore feet and the rain and the slugs were the bad bits, and I thought that the lighthouses and the puffins and the sea-breezes were the good bits.

But now, looking backwards, I understand it perfectly. They were *all* good bits.

I close my eyes and lean back in my seat.

Later, friends will ask, 'What was the highlight?'

That's an easy one.

There were no highlights. Just as there were no lowlights. It was a glorious whole. To isolate any part and say, 'That was the best' or 'that was the worst' would be to diminish the experience, to misunderstand it.

Looking back, I wouldn't change a thing.

Acknowledgements

GRATEFUL THANKS to Mike Harpley for making this book possible, and to Shadi Doostdar for making it a better book than it would have been.